GOOD HOUSEKEEPING
MICROWAVE
HANDBOOK

GOOD HOUSEKEEPING

MICROWAVE HANDBOOK

EBURY PRESS
LONDON

At the time of going to press, it has been recommended by the
Ministry of Agriculture, Fisheries and Food that the use of cling
film should be avoided in microwave cooking. When a recipe
requires you to use cling film, you should either cover with a lid
or a plate, leaving a gap to let the steam escape.

Published in 1992 by Ebury Press
an imprint of the Random Century Group
Random Century House
20 Vauxhall Bridge Road
London SW1V 2SA

Eighteenth impression 1993

ISBN 0 09 177014 9

Edited by Laurine Croasdale, Hilary Walden
Designed by Bill Mason, Jerry Goldie
Cookery by Susanna Tee, Janet Smith

Filmest by Advanced Filmsetters (Glasgow) Ltd
Printed in England by Clays Ltd, St Ives plc

CONTENTS

UNDERSTANDING MICROWAVES

The first thing you need to understand about microwave cooking is that it is a *different* method of cooking to that done in a conventional oven of any other kind. Many people give up on microwaves because they don't understand this. They believe that because they can cook conventionally they should instantly be able to cope with their new appliance.

But microwave cooking is a *technique* that has to be learned. And as with any new technique, it requires time, effort and practice. Few of us who can cook conventionally care to remember early disasters, but virtually everyone has had them and probably will again with their new microwave cooker.

This handbook is designed to take the guesswork out of microwave cooking and if you follow the recipes exactly you will be successful. And once you've mastered the technique you can start to convert your own favourite recipes for this cooking method.

WHAT ARE MICROWAVES?

Microwaves are short wavelength radiation similar to that used in radio and television. They are *not* similar to x-rays and gamma rays and do not build up in the body. In a microwave cooker the microwaves are produced by a component called the *magnetron* which is housed inside the cooker but not visible to the user.

Microwaves are attracted to water molecules present in food and heat it by causing them to vibrate millions of times a second, producing heat on the same principles as rubbing your hands together. Microwaves enter the food on all exposed surfaces which is why it's important to arrange food correctly and use suitable containers (see page 12).

Microwaves penetrate food to a depth of only about 5 cm (2 inches); after that further cooking of foods denser than this is done by conducted heat passing through them. Microwaves do *not*, contrary to some popular theories, cook food from the inside out.

THE ADVANTAGES OF MICROWAVE COOKING

● **Speedy** Microwave cookers heat food more quickly than any conventional oven and are economical in that they use less energy. All domestic microwave cookers run off a 13 amp socket outlet and can be sited anywhere convenient.

- **Clean** With microwave cooking there is no risk of foods burning on to the cooker walls as they do not become hot in the way that the surfaces of a conventional oven do. In addition most foods are cooked covered and so remain in their containers. (See also **Cleaning**, page 14.)

- **Smell free** Because food is contained within the cooker cavity (and usually also in a covered dish), smells are kept to a minimum — useful in flats and bedsitters particularly.

- **Less washing up** It is often possible to microwave food in a serving container or on the plate from which it is to be eaten. This reduces the kind of washing up required when saucepans and metal oven dishes are used.

- **Thawing** Thawing can be done quickly in a microwave cooker, saving hours in the fridge or kitchen and removing the need for too much forward planning. You can decide, a short time before a meal, what currently frozen food you want to eat and how many people to feed.

- **Nutritionally sound** Many foods retain more nutrients than when cooked conventionally because the cooking times are so short and there is little or no added water. Particular examples are fish and vegetables.

- **Easy to use** Once you have mastered the controls and cooking techniques, microwave cookers are extremely easy to use. Basic models are especially suitable for older children, elderly and disabled people who are perhaps just cooking for one and don't want to spend a lot of time in the kitchen.

- **Cool** Unlike conventional ovens, microwave cookers don't produce external heat and so can be used anywhere that is convenient such as a dining room or bedsitter.

MICROWAVE SAFETY

There is no need to be concerned about the safety of microwave cookers. They are built to very high standards and operate only when the door is closed so that there is no risk of the microwaves escaping from the cavity. The door is fitted with special locks, seals and safety cut-out switches which prevent the production of microwaves if a problem occurs, such as a piece of food or cooking film becoming stuck in the door seal.

Although over the years 'scare' stories have surfaced there is no evidence that anyone, anywhere in the world, has been harmed by using a microwave cooker, and in terms of kitchen safety they offer considerably less risk than, say, sharp knives or whirling blades in a machine such as a coffee grinder.

When you choose your microwave cooker check that it carries the BEAB (British Electro-technical Approvals Board) mark, *see WHERE*, and that it conforms to BS (British Standard) 3456. This means that the model has been tested randomly and regularly for both electrical safety and microwave leakage.

When preparing food in a microwave cooker it is perfectly safe – and frequently necessary – to stand in front of it so that you can see if stirring is needed or something is likely to boil over. Microwave door seals are tested 100,000 times before being declared safe so don't feel you have to stand back from the model.

However, you do need to take care to keep the door seal and hinges clean and avoid leaning on the door or banging it shut. Most manufacturers recommend that your model should be checked on a regular basis (usually every one or two years) to make sure that everything is working properly. And if you have had a fire in your microwave or it has been bashed around a bit (perhaps because you had to move it somewhere) it would be sensible to have it checked for possible leakage. You will have to pay the manufacturer's engineer but this is a safer check than buying a cheap leakage detector and doing the job yourself. Tests have shown that these products are not reliable and can allow you to think things are all right when they are not – and *vice versa*.

It is important *never* to switch on your microwave cooker when there is no food in it to attract the microwaves. The waves will bounce around the empty cavity and can damage the magnetron. If you have small children who might fiddle with the controls and possibly switch the appliance on, train yourself always to keep a glass of water in the cooker cavity so that the microwaves can be attracted to it.

Note

If slight microwave leakage *is* occurring, people fitted with early versions of cardiac pacemakers should ask their GP's advice as to whether it will be affected.

TYPES OF MICROWAVE COOKER

You need to think carefully before buying a microwave cooker since there is a wide variety of features to choose from. If you select a very basic model you may eventually wish you had some extra features, while if you choose a more sophisticated machine you and members of your household may find it difficult to master. All the recipes in this book can be prepared in a basic microwave cooker.

POWER OUTPUT

This varies from model to model. Most are now 650 Watts and recipes in this book use the following settings:

HIGH refers to 100% full power output of 600–700 Watts

MEDIUM refers to 60% of full power

LOW is 35% of full power.

If your cooker has a lower power output than this

- **add approximately 10–15 seconds** per minute for a 600 watt oven
- **add approximately 15–20 seconds** per minute for a 500 watt oven.

If your cooker has a higher output you will need to reduce cooking times accordingly.

TYPE OF COOKER

Microwave only cookers come as free-standing or built-in/built-under models. A free-standing one is usually sited on a worktop (where it will reduce working space) but could also be placed on a trolley or sideboard or wall mounted. Note that it is *not* a good idea to move a microwave cooker around unless it is absolutely essential. An accidental knock against something might cause damage to the magnetron.

Built-in cookers may be sited above or below a conventional oven or somewhere separate in the kitchen. Make sure you choose somewhere that is comfortable for you to check or stir food.

Combination microwave cookers combine the facility for microwave-only cooking with conventional (usually convection) cooking. You can therefore use them as a microwave cooker, a small conventional oven or with both types of cooking together which is not as fast as microwave-only cooking but does produce browning and crisping. In a small household or kitchen a combination cooker can cope with most household needs provided you also have a hob and so long as you don't do a lot of entertaining. They can be sited in the same way as microwave-only cookers.

But most people use their microwave or combination cooker as a back-up to a conventional cooker, getting the different benefits from the different types of cooking.

COOKER FEATURES

Controls Are usually the touch type although some models still have mechanical knobs and dials. Look at the controls carefully before you buy; some are more complex than others although most people have no problem after a bit of practice.

Turntable/stirrer In order to spread the microwaves around more evenly, some models come supplied with a turntable which turns the food in its container so that it is exposed to as much penetration as possible. Others have built-in stirrers which circulate the microwaves around the food.

Memory This allows you to programme the cooker in advance, perhaps to start cooking while you are out.

Auto-cooking On some models this works on weight. You programme the weight and food type into the machine which then cooks it for the appropriate time. On others the feature works on moisture and stops cooking when the appropriate level is reached.

Light All models come with an interior light which remains on during cooking and allows you to view food through the door.

Vents These are designed to allow moisture to escape from the oven during cooking. Check where they are on a model so you can be sure that they won't be blocked in the position you intend for it.

MICROWAVE COOKING UTENSILS

There are some materials that can't be used in a microwave cooker because they deflect the microwaves so they don't reach the food. This is true of metals. Other materials are not suitable because they trap microwaves within them, allowing only a few to reach the food thus slowing down the cooking process. This may be fine if you want lengthy cooking in order to tenderise a tough cut of meat (although where available most people would choose to use a conventional hob or oven for this) but it does reduce the speed and efficiency of standard microwave cooking.

A material which tends to trap microwaves is earthenware which contains a certain amount of metal. You can check how suitable a container is for microwave cooking by half filling it with water and using the highest setting for about one minute. If the water is hot and the top of the container cool, the microwaves are getting through and the container is suitable. If both water and dish are warm it is safe for microwave use but will increase cooking times. If the dish is hot and the water cool, too many microwaves are being trapped in the material and it is not suitable for microwave cooking.

SHAPES AND SIZES

The way microwaves bounce around the cooker cavity makes certain shapes and sizes of dish better to use.

Round containers are preferable to square and oval ones because they lack the corners and narrow ends in which microwaves can cluster and overcook food. Ring moulds are particularly good as they allow microwaves to reach the food surface from the inner ring as well as the outside. If you don't own a ring mould you can make your own by placing a glass tumbler in the centre of a round container.

Straight-sided dishes allow food to cook more quickly than those with sloping sides and shallow dishes provide a bigger food surface area for the microwaves to penetrate. Always use a container that you can lift comfortably when it is full of bubbling food and bear in mind that liquids such as soup will boil up and need space for this. Ideally no food should come more than two-thirds up the sides of its container.

CONTAINER MATERIALS

You may want to buy special microwave ware for your cooker or you may already own enough containers made of suitable material. The following materials are all suitable for certain microwave purposes:

Ceramic Often designed specially for microwaves.

China and pottery Standard glazed household china and pottery can be used for microwaving (although do the test above on hand-made pottery which may contain too many metal particles). Unglazed china and pottery are porous and absorb moisture which attracts microwaves into the material and away from the food. Unglazed clay chicken and fish bricks are good for long slow cooking. Soak them well first and if they dry out add more *warm* water. Cold water may cause the brick to crack. Fine bone china should be used for only short periods. Anything decorated with a metal trim should not be used.

Foil Should be used with care as too much can cause arcing (a flash of flame) that might damage the magnetron or cause a fire. Foil is safe in small quantities, to protect the tail end of a fish or thin end of a chop from cooking too quickly.

If using foil containers these should be at least two-thirds full and no deeper than 20 mm with a large surface area. Do *not* use foil-laminated board lids.

Glass Cooks well in a microwave although cut glass and lead crystal should not be used. Glass cookware such as measuring jugs and mixing bowls are useful in the early stages of food preparation, eg warming liquid or frying onions.

Paper Can be used for short periods. If using paper plates they should be white (colour might run into the food) and uncoated (wax and plastic coatings may melt). White paper napkins can be used, for example to line a bread basket. Greaseproof and kitchen paper are useful when put under bread or pastries to prevent them becoming soggy and as a covering when cooking fatty foods to prevent them spattering.

Plastics As a rough guide, rigid plastics are usually safe in a microwave while soft ones are not. Unless you are using a plastic which is guaranteed microwave safe, do the water test above. Note that Melamine absorbs microwaves and prevents food cooking.

There are special durable plastics specifically designed for microwave cooking. Some can be used in a conventional oven as well while others can tolerate only a certain level of heat. **Filled polypropylene** withstands temperatures up to only 140°C so is suitable just for reheating and some low temperature cooking. **Polysulfone** withstands up to 180°C and remains cool. It doesn't stain or absorb odours and is unbreakable. **Thermoset polyester** withstands up to around 210°C and remains cool. It doesn't stain easily and is shatterproof.

Plastic freezer bags and freezer containers can be used for thawing or short reheating. Boiling bags and roasting bags are safe to use provided you tie them with string or plastic ties, *not* metal ones. Always prick a bag before cooking to allow steam to escape or it may burst.

Cling film is excellent for covering foods but should be pierced or slightly folded back to prevent it billowing up and then collapsing and sticking to the food.

Wood, wicker and straw baskets These can be used for brief periods of reheating but will dry out and crack if exposed to microwaves for too long. Wood can be reconditioned if this happens with a light coating of vegetable oil, rubbed in well.

MICROWAVE ACCESSORIES

There are some useful specialist items which make certain types of microwave cooking easier. You may need none or only some of them, depending on what you use your appliance for.

Browning dish or skillet Made of specially coated ceramic, this will produce browning on foods that you would otherwise grill or fry. Can be bulky to store and is not essential if you have a grill or combination oven.

Defrosting rack Comes with a built-in drip tray and is excellent for defrosting meat and cooking dense foods which benefit from microwaves being able to penetrate from underneath.

Vented plate cover and plate stackers The cover saves the use of cling film and kitchen paper as it can be washed and reused. Stackers allow you to cook with plates of food stacked one above the other.

Roasting rack Has a ridged surface which allows microwaves to circulate all round the food and prevents things like joints of meat sitting in their own juices or fat.

Thermometer A special microwave thermometer can be placed in meat or poultry while it is cooking and allows you to see what stage it's at through the door. Some ovens have built-in temperature probes which cause the oven to switch off when a pre-set temperature is reached or reduce the power level to keep the food warm until required.

CLEANING YOUR MICROWAVE COOKER

It is important to keep the interior of your microwave cooker clean so that it works efficiently. If you allow particles of food to build up within it, the microwaves will be attracted to them as well as what is being cooked and the cooking process will be slowed down.

It is also vital (see **Safety**, page 7) to keep the door seal and hinges clean so that the appliance will work in the first place.

Because food does not burn on the surfaces in the way it does in a conventional oven, cleaning is straightforward (although combination ovens suffer the same level of soil as conventional ones when used in their combination or conventional-only mode).

Ideally, wipe out the cavity with a warm, damp cloth wrung out of a mild detergent solution each time you use it or at the end of each day.

If there is stuck-on soil (or the smell you may get after cooking something strong like fish), place a suitable bowl of water to which you have added a few drops of lemon juice in the cavity and heat to boiling point. This will produce steam which condenses on the surfaces and softens any deposits (as well as neutralising any smells). Once clean, wipe dry with a soft cloth or kitchen paper. Do *not* use abrasive cleaners which could damage the interior and *never* use a knife blade or sharp item to scrape off any deposits. Your manufacturer's handbook will give detailed advice on cleaning and suitable products. Removable parts such as turntable, shelf and so on can either be washed up in the normal way in the sink or may be suitable for putting in a dishwasher.

COOKING TECHNIQUES

STIRRING AND TURNING

With microwave cooking it is important to make sure the food cooks evenly and the best way of doing this is to stir and turn the food unless this will spoil its appearance or texture.

As the outside of the food begins to cook first with the inside of the food relying on the slower conduction of heat, it is necessary to equalise out the cooking of liquids and moist foods by stirring from the outside in towards the centre. With solid foods, such as cakes, it is the container that is turned. If the oven is not fitted with a turntable or stirrers turn the container through 90° (a quarter turn) or 180° (a half turn) several times during cooking. Site items off the centre of the turntable to ensure maximum penetration of microwaves. Even if your oven has a turntable, it is advisable to turn cakes to ensure even cooking. Some foods, such as joints of meat, large potatoes and whole cauliflower, should be turned *over* as well during cooking and items such as chops and steaks should be turned over when being thawed.

COVERING

A covering prevents the surface of moist foods from drying out and speeds up the cooking of casseroles, steamed puddings, fish and vegetables by trapping moisture underneath the cover. It also allows the minimum of liquid to be used for items such as vegetables and fruit, so preserving their nutrients and flavour.

The lid can be of any material that is suitable for use in a microwave cooker but if cling film, a plastic bag, boil-in-the-bag, or roasting bag is used, make a slit or hole in it to prevent balooning, bursting and sticking to the food. It will also allow steam to escape. When using a lid, only three-quarters cover the dish. If the food has to be stirred, fold back one corner of a cling film covering so that it can easily be stirred.

Take care when removing either a rigid lid or cling film. Open it away from you as there will be a gush of hot, moist air that can cause a nasty scald.

Cover fatty items that are likely to spatter, such as bacon, with absorbent kitchen paper as this absorbs the fat. Greaseproof paper is useful for covering items such as poached whole pears that are a difficult shape. Unevenly shaped foods, such as chicken joints, have to be partially covered during cooking to prevent thinner areas becoming overcooked. A very small piece of foil wrapped closely over the food, shiny side in, is used for this.

Bread and pastries are not covered because they do not require moist cooking but benefit from having a piece of kitchen paper placed underneath to absorb moisture and prevent sogginess.

ARRANGEMENT OF FOOD

The correct arrangement of food is necessary to make sure that it cooks, thaws or reheats evenly. Place thicker or more dense areas outermost so they are nearer the source of the microwaves with thinner, more delicate areas near the centre, overlapping them or covering with a small piece of foil.

When cooking several items, such as small cakes, jacket potatoes, baked apples or biscuits, arrange then in a circle on a plate or directly on the oven shelf to allow the microwaves to penetrate from the centre as well as the outside. If this is not possible, rearrange the items during the cooking, thawing or reheating, placing the outer items in the centre and vice versa and removing items as soon as they are cooked, thawed or feel warm.

The more surface area that can be exposed to the microwaves the quicker, and more even the cooking, thawing or reheating will be.

BROWNING

Because of the speed and the way in which microwave energy cooks, food cooked in a microwave cooker will not be brown, with the exception of joints and poultry that require more than 20 minutes. These will be brown but they will not be crisp and will look a little different from conventionally cooked dishes.

There are many ways of giving food a more traditionally browned appearance if necessary. Meats and poultry can be browned under a browning element, in a browning dish, under a grill or in a frying pan. They can also be sprinkled with paprika pepper, browned breadcrumbs or brushed with brown, tomato, Tabasco, soy or Worcestershire sauce or glazed with honey, apricot jam or marmalade.

STANDING TIME

All food continues to cook after it has been removed from a microwave cooker, or the power switches off, not by the action of microwaves but by the conduction of heat. The period during which this happens is known as the 'standing time' and during it the heat will equalise throughout the food. The time this takes depends on the density and size of the food and very often it will be no longer than the time taken to serve the dish. However, for larger joints of meat and poultry it may be as long as 15–20 minutes.

The standing time must always be taken into account when estimating the cooking of foods but if in doubt always undercook rather than overcook and test it at the end of the standing period. Food can always be given a few extra seconds in the cooker if necessary.

SEASONING

Salt draws out moisture and has a toughening effect on meats, fish and vegetables so do not add salt directly to foods without any liquid until the cooking is complete. As the food cooks so quickly there is not enough time for the flavour of seasoning to be absorbed thoroughly into the food so season lightly. The level can always be adjusted at the end of the cooking.

FACTORS AFFECTING COOKING TIMES

The time that food takes to cook, thaw or reheat in a microwave cooker will vary according to the following factors.

COMPOSITION

Food with a high moisture content will take longer to cook or reheat than drier foods, whilst those which are high in fat or sugar, cook or reheat more rapidly than those which are low in these ingredients. Jam, marmalade and other sugary coatings on cakes, puddings or tarts will heat up much more quickly than the rest of the food and can become extremely hot so do not attempt to eat them straight from the microwave cooker. Bone conducts heat so meat on the bone will cook more quickly than if it has been boned, but it will not cook evenly.

DENSITY AND TEXTURE

Light, open-textured foods will cook and reheat more quickly than more dense items. For example, minced meat will cook more quickly than the same weight of solid meat.

SIZE OF FOOD

Several small pieces of food will cook more quickly than the same amount cooked in one piece. A joint requires longer cooking time if left whole than diced meat but with small pieces it is important to make sure that they are cut to the same size so that they cook at the same speed.

QUANTITY OF FOOD

The larger the quantity of food the longer it will take to cook, but doubling the quantity does not necessarily mean doubling the time. As a rough guide allow approximately one third to one half extra time when doubling the amount of food. Similarly, a reduction in the amount of food calls for a reduction in the cooking time.

TEMPERATURE

The colder food is the longer it will take to heat up. The times given in the recipes are for foods at a normal temperature. Ideally, chilled food should stand for about an hour before cooked or reheated to allow it to warm up. If this is not possible, add a little extra to the cooking times, erring on the cautious side, so that the food does not overcook.

SIZE, SHAPE AND MATERIAL OF THE CONTAINER

For the ways in which the choice of container can affect the cooking times, see pages 11 and 12.

THAWING

The rapid thawing of frozen foods and the absence of the need to plan ahead are major points in favour of microwave cookers. When food is thawed smaller ice crystals will melt first, followed by larger ones. Therefore, if the thawing is too rapid the parts of the food with the smallest ice crystals or the thinner parts, will start to cook before the rest of the food has thawed.

A 'defrost' control will take care of the thawing automatically but if your oven is not fitted with one gentle thawing can be accomplished easily by switching the power on and off in bursts of about 30 seconds. Should the food start to thaw unevenly, cover the area that is in danger of cooking with a small piece of foil, shiny side inwards. If possible, turn foods over during thawing, separate items such as chops and steaks as soon as possible, shake or fork small fruit and vegetables apart and stir liquid or semi-liquid items such as casseroles, breaking them up with a fork at the beginning of the thawing. Cover foods where necessary (see page 15) using absorbent kitchen paper for breads and pastries.

Put foods into containers of an appropriate size and shape — stews, casseroles, sauces and other liquid items will thaw more evenly if put into a deep dish that keeps the contents together. If the dish is too large the liquid will flow and start to heat before the rest of the food has begun to thaw.

Replace metal ties on polythene bags with string or plastic ties and transfer food from aluminium foil trays into more suitable containers. Open cartons and any other containers with lids and slit or pierce plastic bags or packets. Foods with skins, such as frankfurter sausages, should also be pierced.

If poultry is thawed in its original plastic bag, pour off the liquid as soon as it melts and accumulates in the bottom of the bag.

The times given in the charts (see Glossary, page 86) are intended as a guide only, as the temperature inside freezers vary and so the temperature of frozen food will vary. Always underestimate thawing time, and take into account the thawing that will take place during the final standing time.

REHEATING

Foods can be reheated very easily in a matter of minutes without great loss of nutrients or colour, and little risk of food drying out. Furthermore, an entire course for a meal can be reheated on the serving plate, so saving on washing up. When doing this, keep the height of the various items as even as possible and arrange the more dense and thicker items towards the outside of the plate.

Follow the same procedure as when reheating foods conventionally and cover moist items such as meat casseroles to prevent them drying out. Stir the food occasionally to ensure it heats through evenly. Items that cannot be stirred should be turned (see Stirring and Turning, page 15).

Cover slices of meat, which should be thin rather than thick as these will heat through more quickly, with gravy or a sauce. Place cooked pastry items such as flans, individual pastries, and breads on absorbent kitchen paper as this absorbs moisture during reheating and prevents the bottom becoming soggy.

As microwaves are attracted to moist fillings liquid will heat more quickly than, say, pieces of meat. As a result, the steam that is produced will be absorbed into the pastry covering. However, it can easily be crisped up by popping it under a hot grill or browning element. Reheating is extremely quick so small items should not be left unattended and all items should, if possible, be undercooked initially to avoid overcooking when reheated. This particularly applies to vegetables. Fibrous vegetables may toughen whilst starchy ones will quickly dry out unless covered with cling film.

To test when food is ready, feel the container beneath it – if it feels warm the food will be hot. With pastry items such as fruit pies the outer pastry should feel just warm because the filling, which has a high sugar and water content, will become very hot if cooked long enough for the pastry to feel very hot. The temperature of pastry and filling will equalise after a few minutes standing time.

COMBINING MICROWAVE AND CONVENTIONAL COOKING

A microwave cooker is an excellent back up to a conventional oven or hob. It can make many food preparation tasks quicker and easier.

- Partly cook chicken portions and small cuts of meat ready for browning and crisping on a barbecue or under a conventional grill.

- To save washing up a saucepan, melt butter or chocolate for mousses or cakes in a small bowl before adding the remaining ingredients and beating together well.

- Soften butter to a spreading consistency by microwaving on MEDIUM – 225 g (8 oz) will take 30 seconds.
  Soften sugar that has become hard in its original wrapping on HIGH for 30–40 seconds.

- Restore the texture of syrup or honey that has crystallised by microwaving on HIGH for 1–2 minutes in a non-metal container without a lid.

- Plump dried fruits by covering with water and microwaving on HIGH for 5 minutes. Stir, leave to stand for 5 minutes then drain well and dry on absorbent paper.

- To toast flaked almonds place them on a large non-metal plate and microwave on HIGH for 8–10 minutes, stirring frequently.

- Brown desiccated coconut in a roasting bag on HIGH for 5 minutes.

- To remove the skins and brown hazelnuts microwave them in a single layer on absorbent kitchen paper for 30 seconds on HIGH, rub off the skins and return to the oven until just golden.

- To roast chestnuts, slit the skins with a sharp knife and microwave on HIGH for 3 minutes per 225 g (8 oz).

- For quick roasting potatoes, joints or whole poultry start the cooking in a microwave oven then brown and crisp them in hot fat or oil in a conventional oven or under a grill.

- Use a microwave oven for speedily cooking the basic ingredients for breadcrumb and cheese-topped savoury dishes as well as crunchy or crumble-topped desserts then brown and crisp the surface under a conventional grill or in a conventional oven.

- Prepare the fillings for pastry cases in a microwave oven while the pastry is baking in a conventional oven.

MENU PLANNING

FAMILY MEAL FOR FOUR

**Cream of mushroom soup
(see page 34)
Bread rolls
...
Italian meatballs (see page 55)
Spaghetti (see chart page 91)
Green salad
...
Stuffed baked apples
(see page 67)**

1¼ hours before serving
Make the soup up to the end of step 4. Make the meatballs and transfer to a serving dish. Set aside but do not refrigerate. Prepare the cooking apples and place in individual serving dishes, but do not cook. Cover and set aside.

Prepare a green salad and a dressing but do not toss them together.

Cook 350 g (12 oz) spaghetti as instructed on page 91. Leave to stand, covered. While the spaghetti is standing, finish cooking the soup as directed in step 5. It may take slightly longer than stated in the recipe because it has cooled.

When serving
Place four bread rolls in a wicker serving basket or on a piece of absorbent kitchen paper and microwave on HIGH for 20–30 seconds until just warmed through. Serve the soup with the rolls.

While eating the soup, reheat the meatballs on HIGH for 5–8 minutes until heated through.

When ready to serve the main course, drain the spaghetti, turn into a serving dish and toss together with a knob of butter and 15 ml (1 tbsp) vegetable oil and plenty of black pepper. Re-cover and microwave on HIGH for 2–3 minutes.

While the spaghetti is reheating, toss the salad with the dressing.

Serve the meatballs with the spaghetti and the salad.

Cook the apples as instructed in steps 4 and 5 while eating the main course.

INFORMAL SUPPER FOR SIX

**Garlic bread
Chilli con carne (see page 48)
Cooked rice (see page 91)
...
Strawberry Fool (see page 69)
or
Cheese and biscuits
and fresh fruit**

The day before
Make the chilli con carne to the end of step 2. Cool quickly, cover and refrigerate overnight. Prepare the Strawberry Fool.

30 minutes before serving
Cook 350 g (12 oz) rice as instructed on page 91. Rinse and drain and turn into a serving dish.

25

30 minutes before serving (cont.)

Meanwhile, prepare the garlic bread; cream 100 g (4 oz) chopped butter until soft, then stir in two skinned and crushed garlic cloves. Season with salt and pepper. Cut a French loaf into thick diagonal slices. Spread the slices on both sides with the butter then, reshape the loaf. Wrap in greaseproof paper.

Reheat the chilli con carne on LOW for 10 minutes, then on HIGH for a further 5–10 minutes until bubbling and hot. Continue as recipe step 3.

To serve

Leave the chilli to stand, covered, for 5 minutes, while reheating the rice.

Cover the rice and reheat on HIGH for 5–6 minutes or until hot, stirring thoroughly with a fork several times during the cooking.

When the rice is hot, microwave the garlic bread on HIGH for 1½ minutes until hot. Finish the meal with Strawberry Fool or a selection of cheeses and biscuits and some fresh fruit.

QUICK FAMILY SUPPER FOR FOUR

Spicy pork chops (see page 45)
Jacket potatoes (see page 28)
Frozen peas
French beans
...
Hot sherried grapefruit
(see page 66)

The night before

Prepare the chops up to step 2 and leave to marinate overnight in the refrigerator.

50 minutes before serving

Prepare the grapefruit to the end of step 2 and set aside.

Scrub four 175 g (6 oz) potatoes and prick with a fork. Microwave on HIGH for 12–14 minutes or until cooked (check by pricking with a fork); wrap in foil and leave to stand or put unwrapped into a hot oven to crisp skins.

Meanwhile, top and tail 350 g (12 oz) French beans and cut into 2.5 cm (1 inch) lengths. Put into a roasting bag with 30 ml (2 tbsp) water. Put 350 g (12 oz) peas into another roasting bag. When the potatoes are cooked, finish cooking the chops as in step 3. Leave to stand while cooking the vegetables.

Microwave the beans and peas on HIGH for 6–7 minutes. Drain.

Unwrap the potatoes and microwave on HIGH for 1–2 minutes, if necessary, to warm them through. Microwave the chops on HIGH for 1 minute, if necessary, to warm them through. Serve the chops with the potatoes and vegetables.

For the dessert, cook the grapefruit as in step 3.

EASY SAMPLE RECIPES

The following recipes demonstrate many microwave cookery techniques.

SCRAMBLED EGGS

SERVES 2
4 eggs
60 ml (4 tbsp) milk
25 g (1 oz) butter or margarine
*   (optional)*
salt and pepper
hot buttered toast, to serve

1 Put all the ingredients in a medium mixing bowl and whisk together with a balloon whisk.

All the ingredients are mixed in a medium bowl rather than a saucepan and a whisk is used rather than a wooden spoon. You can use a serving bowl to cook the eggs in or a microware container. One of the great features of microwave cookery is that many containers which are not suitable for conventional cooking can be used.

2 Microwave on HIGH for $1\frac{1}{2}$ minutes until the mixture just begins to set around the edge of the bowl.

Open the door and take out the bowl. You will notice that the bowl is not hot. This is because the microwaves pass through the bowl into the food. You will also notice that the eggs have started to set around the edge of the bowl, but they are still very soft in the centre. This is because food on the outside of the dish cooks more quickly in a microwave oven. Therefore mixtures such as this should be stirred from the outside inwards.

3 Whisk vigorously to incorporate the set egg mixture. Microwave on HIGH for a further $1\frac{1}{2}$–2 minutes, whisking every 30 seconds, until the eggs are just set. Remember that the mixture will continue to cook a little after it has been removed from the oven. Serve on hot buttered toast.

These cooking times are a guide as they vary according to the temperature of the eggs at the beginning of the cooking, e.g. room temperature or taken straight from the refrigerator. Eggs cooked in this way in the microwave oven are much lighter than when cooked conventionally. The bowl will be slightly hot at the end of the cooking time because the heat from the cooked eggs will be conducted to the bowl. But as the bowl is not heated directly, the egg will not stick to it and so the bowl will be easy to clean. The oven cavity will not be hot because of the very short cooking time.

COOKING BACON

6 slices bacon, rinded

1 Snip the rind with scissors to prevent it curling up during cooking. Lay in a single layer on a microwave roasting rack or large flat plate. Cover with a piece of absorbent kitchen paper.

Bacon is easily and successfully cooked in the microwave and is a good example of special techniques needed for microwave cookery. It must be snipped and laid in a single layer to prevent it curling and so cooking unevenly. A microwave roasting rack is useful for cooking bacon and other meats in the microwave because it raises them above their juices during cooking. Bacon and other fatty foods should be covered with absorbent kitchen paper to prevent fat spattering in the cooker and diverting some of the microwaves away from the food.

2 Microwave bacon on HIGH for 5–6 minutes until cooked. Two slices will take $2-2\frac{1}{2}$ minutes, four slices about $4-4\frac{1}{2}$ minutes. Pat off any excess fat with absorbent kitchen paper if necessary. Remove the paper quickly to prevent it sticking to the bacon.

The cooking times are a guide as they can vary according to the thickness as well as the starting temperature of the bacon.

Bacon cooked in this way in the microwave will be slightly browned and crisped. This is because of the high fat content of the bacon. The bacon can be cooked on a plate that can be used as a serving plate, so reducing washing up to a minimum!

JACKET POTATOES

four 175 g (6 oz) old potatoes

1 Wash and scrub the potatoes. Prick the skin all over with a fork. Arrange in the oven in a circle with a space in the centre, on absorbent kitchen paper.

It is important to prick foods with skins or tough membranes to prevent a build up of pressure which could cause the food to explode.

Potatoes should be arranged in a circle in the oven leaving a space in the centre for more evenly cooked results. The space in the centre provides a greater area of outer surfaces and allows the microwaves to act more efficiently in the oven.

Kitchen paper helps to absorb any moisture produced while cooking.

2 Microwave on HIGH for 6 minutes then turn the potatoes over and cook for a further 6–8 minutes until the potatoes feel soft when squeezed gently.

One potato will take 4 minutes. Two potatoes will take 6–7 minutes.

Thick foods such as potatoes should be turned round, if the oven does not have a turntable, and over during cooking because microwaves only penetrate the food to a depth of about 5 cm (2 inches).

Jacket potatoes are a good example of the speed of microwave cookery, but the result is not exactly the same as that obtained when they are cooked conventionally. The skin of the potato will not be crisp. Microwaving is a moist form of cooking so the surfaces of 'baked' foods cannot become crisp, brown.

CHICKEN DRUMSTICKS

15 ml (1 tbsp) vegetable oil
4 chicken drumsticks

1 Preheat a large browning dish according to the manufacturer's instructions, adding oil for the last 30 seconds. If you do not have a browning dish, put the oil in a large shallow dish and microwave on HIGH for 1–2 minutes, until hot.

A browning dish enables foods to be browned in the microwave cooker, but they must be preheated to be effective. It is possible to cook drumsticks without a browning dish but they will not be brown.

2 Without removing the dish from the oven, place the drumsticks in the hot oil, arranging them in a circle, with the thinner, bonier ends towards the centre. If using an ordinary dish, arrange in the same way.

It is important to put the food on to the hot browning dish as soon as it is heated or it will have cooled and will not be as effective. Drumsticks, and other irregularly-shaped foods, should be arranged with the more quickly cooked, thinner or more porous parts towards the centre of the dish. Cooking is most successful when the food is arranged with an empty space in the middle so there is a greater surface area for the microwaves to penetrate.

3 Microwave on HIGH for 6–9 minutes until cooked. Turn the chicken over once during cooking.

It is important to turn drumsticks over during the cooking because microwaves penetrate only to a depth of about 5 cm (2 inches). Turning during cooking ensures more even and efficient cooking. When poultry is cooked the juices should run clear without any trace of pinkish colour. Larger pieces of poultry should be left to stand after cooking and then checked for pink juices.

SMALL CAKES

MAKES ABOUT 18
150 g (5 oz) butter or margarine
100 g (4 oz) caster sugar
2 eggs
75 g (3 oz) self raising flour
25 g (1 oz) cocoa powder
15–30 ml (1–2 tbsp) milk
100 g (4 oz) plain chocolate,
*   broken into small pieces*

1 Cut 100 g (4 oz) of the butter into 2.5 cm (1 inch) pieces and put in a large bowl. Microwave on HIGH for 10–15 seconds until slightly softened but not melted.

Here the microwave saves time and energy by softening the fat so making it much easier to beat. Cutting the fat into small pieces before microwaving reduces the melting time by exposing a greater surface area to the microwaves.

2 Stir in the sugar, eggs, flour and cocoa powder and beat well.

Cakes and pastries do not brown in the microwave. Icing will disguise the pale surface but if they are to be served uniced, the addition of cocoa, as here, or ginger, spices, brown sugar or wholemeal flour, will produce an acceptable result.

3 Add enough milk to make a very soft dropping consistency.

A very soft consistency is needed because cakes cooked in the microwave are more successful if the mixture is softer than a conventional cake mixture. This is because they are cooked partly by the steam that is produced by the liquid during cooking.

4 Put 6 paper cases into a microwave muffin pan or into 6 tea cups without a gilt trim. Fill the paper cases one-third full with cake mixture.

It is better to cook just a few cakes at a time in the microwave oven as they will cook more quickly and evenly (time is still saved because they cook so quickly). Only fill one-third full because cakes rise much higher when cooked in the microwave. As when cooking potatoes, cakes should be arranged in a circle for even cooking.

5 Microwave on HIGH for 1 minute until the surface of the cakes appears almost dry.

It is important to cook cakes for the minimum of time. If over-cooked they will be very dry and unpalatable. When cooked, cakes will still appear moist on the surface. Do not continue cooking at this stage. They will continue to cook when removed from the oven and left to stand. This is because when foods are removed from the microwave oven they do not start to cool immediately as with conventional cooking, but continue to cook for some time. Therefore this standing time is an important part of microwave cookery and should not be ignored.

6 Remove the cakes from their containers. Leave to cool on a wire rack.

Microwave cakes are much lighter in texture than conventionally cooked cakes and will have a softer crust than when conventionally baked because it is a moist form of cooking.

7 Place 6 more paper cases in the pan or cups and repeat as above. Then repeat again.

8 When the cakes are cool, put the chocolate in a small bowl. Microwave on LOW for 3–4 minutes until melted, stirring occasionally. Stir in the remaining butter and microwave on HIGH for 1 minute. Spread the icing over the cakes to decorate.

Microwave ovens are ideal for melting chocolate because there is no need to use a pan of steaming water. Chocolate can be melted on HIGH but it is better to use LOW because it easily over-heats and burns. It is important to stir the chocolate occasionally during melting to obtain even melting.

HOT DRINKS

	Amount	Approximate time on HIGH
Milk or water for	1 cup	$1\frac{1}{4}$–$2\frac{3}{4}$ minutes
instant coffee, tea	2 cups	3–$4\frac{1}{4}$ minutes
or cocoa	4 cups	5–$8\frac{1}{2}$ minutes

1 cup/mug = 175 ml (6 fl oz)

1 Fill cup/mug to only three-quarters full. If heating more than one cup, arrange in a circle with space between each one, leaving the centre empty.

When heating liquids in the microwave oven always leave a space between the surface of the liquid and the brim of the cup or container to avoid any spillage as the liquid expands. Add instant coffee, tea-bag or cocoa once the liquid has boiled. Watch drinks through the oven door, especially when heating milk-based liquids which form a skin and quickly boil over. When boiling point is reached, open the oven door to prevent the drink boiling over. Microwave cookers are economical for heating small numbers of individual drinks but for boiling larger quantities of water it is quicker and more economical to use a kettle. This is another example of how microwave cookery utilises serving utensils (i.e. mugs/cups) for cooking in. When heating drinks in cups/mugs the cup/mug will be hot because of heat conduction from the hot liquid, in much the same way as a mug full of conventionally made tea gets hot.

31

SOUPS

Microwave cookers are extremely useful both for preparing soups and for thawing or reheating ones that have already been made. When making a soup in a microwave oven use a deep, round container that allows plenty of room for the expansion of the liquid as it comes to the boil and for it to be stirred, if necessary. If a number of ingredients are used in the soup the various flavours will mingle better if the soup is made in advance, cooled quickly, then reheated when required.

Soups can be reheated in individual bowls, so saving on washing up. Use a Low or Medium setting for soups that have been thickened with eggs or which contain cream, soured cream, seafood, or pulses but use a High setting for all others. Thick soups take longer to reheat than thin or clear ones. Pour soup that is to be frozen into single-portion containers, such as a soup bowl, lined with a freezer bag and fill three-quarters full. Freeze, then remove the container, label and seal the bag. Then, when the soup is to be served, it can be removed from the bag and put straight into the soup bowl.

HEATING CANNED SOUP

1 | Pour the soup into a large jug, individual soup bowls or a soup tureen, diluting if recommended by the manufacturer, e.g. condensed soups.

2 | Cover with cling film, pulling back one corner to allow the steam to escape. Microwave on HIGH until hot. A 435 g (15 oz) can will require 3–4 minutes.

3 | Stir the soup and leave to stand, covered, for a few minutes before serving.

COOKING DEHYDRATED SOUP MIXES

1 | Reconstitute according to the packet instructions in a large jug or bowl which should be no more than two thirds full.

2 | Cover with cling film, pulling back one corner to allow the steam to escape. Microwave on HIGH to bring to the boil; 600–750 ml (1–1¼ pints) takes 6–8 minutes; 1 litre (1¾ pints) takes 8–10 minutes.

3 | Stir and leave to stand, covered, for a few minutes before serving.

CREAMY CHICKEN AND MUSHROOM SOUP

SERVES 3–4

*298 g (10½ oz) can condensed
    chicken soup*
*100 g (4 oz) button mushrooms,
    sliced very thinly*
45–60 ml (3–4 tbsp) single cream
*45–60 ml (3–4 tbsp) chopped
    fresh chives*

1 Dilute the soup as directed on the can then stir in the mushrooms. Mix together well then three-quarters fill three or four soup bowls or cups. If they are too full the soup may boil over during cooking.

2 Place the bowls in a circle in the oven and microwave on HIGH for 6–8 minutes until the soup just comes to the boil.

3 Swirl a tablespoon of cream on the top of each bowl, sprinkle with chives and serve.

TOMATO AND PEPPER SOUP

SERVES 4

397 g (14 oz) can tomatoes
200 g (7 oz) can pimientos, drained
15 ml (1 tbsp) vegetable oil
1 garlic clove, skinned and crushed
*1 small onion, skinned and finely
    chopped*
15 ml (1 level tbsp) plain flour
450 ml (¾ pint) chicken stock
salt and pepper
*snipped fresh chives and croûtons,
    to garnish*

1 Purée the tomatoes and pimientos in a blender or food processor, then sieve to remove the seeds.

2 Place the oil, garlic and onion in a large bowl and microwave on HIGH for 5 minutes until slightly softened.

3 Stir in the flour then gradually stir in the stock. Add the tomato and pimiento purée and season well with salt and pepper.

4 Microwave on HIGH for 8–10 minutes until thickened, stirring frequently. Serve, garnished with chives and croûtons.

LENTIL AND BACON SOUP

SERVES 6

*100 g (4 oz) streaky bacon, rinded
    and chopped*
*25 g (1 oz) butter or margarine,
    diced*
100 g (4 oz) red lentils
*2 leeks, trimmed, finely chopped
    and washed*
*2 carrots, peeled and finely
    chopped*
1 litre (1¾ pints) chicken stock
*30 ml (2 tbsp) chopped fresh
    parsley*
salt and pepper

1 Put the bacon and butter or margarine in a large heatproof bowl and microwave on HIGH for 2 minutes. Add the lentils and toss to coat them in the fat, then add the leeks, carrots and stock.

2 Cover with cling film, pulling back one corner to allow the steam to escape, and microwave on HIGH for 18 minutes until the lentils are cooked. Stir two or three times during cooking.

3 Allow to cool slightly, then purée the soup in a blender or food processor until smooth. Add the parsley, salt and pepper and return the soup to a clean heatproof bowl. Microwave on HIGH for 2–3 minutes until boiling.

CREAM OF MUSHROOM SOUP

SERVES 4–6

50 g (2 oz) butter or margarine
1 small onion, skinned and
    chopped
1 chicken stock cube
225 g (8 oz) button mushrooms,
    sliced
bouquet garni
25 g (1 oz) cornflour
300 ml (½ pint) milk
salt and pepper
50 ml (2 fl oz) single cream

1 Put the butter and chopped onion in a large bowl. Cover with cling film, pulling back one corner to allow the steam to escape. Microwave on HIGH for 5–7 minutes until softened.

2 Dissolve the stock cube in 600 ml (1 pint) boiling water and add to the onion with the sliced mushrooms and bouquet garni. Re-cover and microwave on HIGH for 15–20 minutes.

3 Remove the bouquet garni and either sieve the soup or liquidise it in a blender or food processor until smooth.

4 Blend the cornflour with a little of the milk, then stir in the remaining milk. Stir into the mushroom mixture and re-cover.

5 Microwave on HIGH for about 10 minutes, stirring frequently. Season with salt and pepper, pour into a serving dish and swirl the cream on top.

QUICK ONION SOUP

SERVES 6

25 g (1 oz) butter or margarine
350 g (12 oz) onion, skinned and
    finely sliced
298 ml (10½ oz) can condensed
    consommé
salt and pepper
six 2.5 cm (1 inch) slices French
    bread
50 g (2 oz) Gruyère or Cheddar
    cheese, grated

1 Put the butter in a large bowl and microwave on HIGH for 45 seconds until melted.

2 Add the onions, cover with cling film, pulling back one corner to allow the steam to escape and microwave on HIGH for 8–10 minutes until the onions are very soft, stirring occasionally.

3 Stir in the consommé and 450 ml (¾ pint) water. Season well with salt and pepper. Re-cover with cling film, pulling back one corner to allow the steam to escape and microwave on HIGH for 10 minutes until very hot, stirring occasionally. Leave to stand, covered.

4 Arrange the French bread in a circle on a large flat plate and sprinkle with the cheese. Microwave on HIGH for 1 minute until the cheese melts.

5 Transfer the soup to a warmed soup tureen or individual bowls and float the slices of bread on top. Serve immediately.

WATERCRESS SOUP

SERVES 6

50 g (2 oz) butter or margarine,
  diced
1 large onion, skinned and chopped
2 large bunches of watercress,
  trimmed, washed and chopped
45 ml (3 level tbsp) plain flour
1.1 litres (2 pints) chicken stock
salt and pepper
150 ml (¼ pint) single cream

1 Put the butter into a large heatproof bowl and microwave on HIGH for 1 minute until melted. Add the onions and cover with cling film, pulling back one corner to allow the steam to escape. Microwave on HIGH for 5–7 minutes until the onion softens.

2 Add the watercress, reserving a few sprigs to garnish. Cover and microwave on HIGH for 1–2 minutes. Stir in the flour and microwave on HIGH for 30 seconds. Gradually stir in the stock and season with salt and pepper. Recover and microwave on HIGH for 8 minutes, stirring frequently.

3 Allow the soup to cool for about 5 minutes, then purée in a blender or food processor until smooth.

4 To reheat the soup, return to a clean heatproof bowl and stir in the cream. Microwave on LOW for 6–7 minutes, stirring frequently, until hot but not boiling.
   Serve either hot or well chilled, garnished with the reserved watercress sprigs.

VICHYSSOISE

SERVES 6

15 ml (1 tbsp) vegetable oil
1 medium onion, skinned and
  finely chopped
350 g (12 oz) potatoes, peeled and
  diced
350 g (12 oz) leeks, trimmed and
  finely shredded
750 ml (1¼ pints) chicken stock
salt and pepper
30 ml (2 tbsp) soured or double
  cream
15 ml (1 tbsp) snipped fresh chives

1 Put the oil and onion in a large heatproof bowl and microwave on HIGH for 5–7 minutes until softened. Stir once.

2 Add the potatoes and leeks to the onion. Cover with cling film, pulling back one corner to allow the steam to escape, and microwave on HIGH for 5 minutes, stirring every minute.

3 Add half the stock, re-cover and microwave on HIGH for 4 minutes until boiling.

4 Microwave on HIGH for a further 10 minutes or until the vegetables are soft.

5 Allow to cool for about 5 minutes then purée in a blender or food processor until smooth. Add the remaining stock and season with salt and pepper.

6 To reheat the soup, return it to a clean heatproof bowl and microwave on HIGH for 3 minutes until boiling, stirring occasionally.

7 Stir in the cream then sprinkle over the chives.

SNACKS

Snacks are easy to prepare in a microwave oven and, as they usually require simple, inexpensive ingredients, they are ideal for cooks who are new to microwave cooking and wish to experiment or practise their skills. Many snacks can be made in advance then quickly reheated when required.

The eggs and cheese that form the basis of many snacks are sensitive foods and, as when cooking conventionally, they are easily spoilt by overcooking. Cooking for both should be gentle and quick. Cheese will cook more evenly if grated rather than sliced or diced. To melt cheese, add it just before the end of cooking. Processed cheese cooks even more quickly.

Eggs should not be cooked in their shells. The whites and yolks cook at different speeds, so when poaching or baking, slightly undercook and allow a standing time to complete the process evenly. Only use eggs that are at room temperature and prick the yolks with the point of a sharp knife, a needle or point of a wooden cocktail stick.

EGGS FLORENTINE

SERVES 4

900 g (2 lb) fresh spinach, washed,
    trimmed and coarsely chopped
25 g (1 oz) butter or margarine
45 ml (3 level tbsp) plain flour
1.25 ml (¼ level tsp) mustard
    powder
300 ml (½ pint) milk
100 g (4 oz) Cheddar cheese,
    finely grated
salt and pepper
4 eggs
brown bread and butter, to serve

1 Put the spinach in a large bowl. Cover and microwave on HIGH for 4 minutes until just tender. Leave to stand, covered.

2 Put the butter in a medium bowl and microwave on HIGH for 45 seconds until melted. Stir in the flour and mustard and microwave on HIGH for 30 seconds.

3 Gradually whisk in the milk. Microwave on HIGH for 5 minutes until boiling and thickened, whisking after every minute. Stir in two-thirds of the cheese. Season with salt and pepper.

4 Break the eggs into a microwave muffin pan or bun tray. Gently prick the yolks with a fine knife or needle and microwave on HIGH for 2 minutes or until just set.

5 Drain the spinach thoroughly, place in a flame-proof dish, put the eggs on top and spoon the sauce over. Sprinkle with the reserved cheese and brown under a hot grill.

Serve with brown bread and butter.

CHEESE AND MUSHROOM OMELETTE

SERVES 2

15 g (½ oz) butter or margarine
1 small onion, skinned and thinly
    sliced
50 g (2 oz) mushrooms, sliced
75 g (3 oz) Gruyère or Cheddar
    cheese, grated
3 eggs
30 ml (2 tbsp) milk
15 ml (1 tbsp) chopped fresh
    parsley
salt and pepper

1 Put the butter in a 20.5 cm (8 inch) shallow dish and microwave on HIGH for 30 seconds until melted.

2 Add the onion and mushrooms, cover with cling film with one corner pulled back to allow steam to escape and microwave on HIGH for 3 minutes until softened, stirring once.

3 Beat half of the cheese, the eggs, milk, parsley and salt and pepper together and pour into the dish. Cover loosely with cling film and microwave on LOW for a further 3 minutes, until the omelette is set.

4 Carefully remove the cling film and sprinkle with the remaining cheese.

CHEESE AND POTATO PIE

SERVES 4

900 g (2 lb) potatoes, peeled and
    coarsely grated
1 medium onion, skinned and
    finely chopped
275 g (10 oz) Cheddar cheese,
    coarsely grated
225 g (8 oz) piece of ham, cut into
    1 cm (½ inch) cubes
pinch of grated nutmeg
salt and pepper
25 g (1 oz) butter or margarine,
    diced
50 g (2 oz) fresh breadcrumbs
30 ml (2 tbsp) chopped fresh parsley
green salad, to serve

1 Pat the potatoes dry with absorbent kitchen paper and mix with the onion, cheese and ham. Season well with nutmeg and salt and pepper.

2 Spoon the mixture into a 26.5 cm (10½ inch) shallow round dish and dot with the butter. Cover and microwave on HIGH for 20–25 minutes or until the potato is cooked.

3 Mix the breadcrumbs and parsley together and sprinkle evenly over the top. Place under a hot grill until golden brown
    Serve hot with a green salad.

BAKED BEANS OR SPAGHETTI ON TOAST

SERVES 1

1 slice of bread, toasted
140 g (5 oz) can baked beans or
    spaghetti in tomato sauce

1 Place the hot toast on a serving plate.

2 Spoon the beans or spaghetti on to the toast.

3 Microwave on HIGH for 1–1½ minutes and serve immediately.

NOTE:
Beans may 'pop' during the heating period, so do not overheat them.

ONION COCOTTES

SERVES 4

25 g (1 oz) butter or margarine
2 medium onions, skinned and
    finely chopped
2.5 ml ($\frac{1}{2}$ level tsp) cornflour
salt and pepper
4 eggs
60 ml (4 tbsp) double cream
50 g (2 oz) Cheddar cheese, thinly
    sliced
hot buttered toast, to serve

1   Put the butter in a medium bowl and microwave on HIGH for 45 seconds until melted. Stir in the onions and microwave on HIGH for 5–7 minutes until softened.

2   Blend the cornflour with about 5 ml (1 tsp) water. Stir into the onions and microwave on HIGH for 1 minute. Season with salt and pepper.

3   Divide the mixture between four ramekin dishes and break an egg into each dish. Gently prick each egg yolk with a needle, fine skewer or wooden cocktail stick. Spoon the cream over and top with the cheese. Microwave on HIGH for 4 minutes or until the eggs are just set. Leave to stand for 1–2 minutes. Serve with hot buttered toast.

TUNA FISH CAKES

SERVES 4

2 large potatoes, total weight
    about 350 g (12 oz)
25 g (1 oz) butter or margarine
1 small onion, skinned and finely
    chopped
198 g (7 oz) can tuna fish, drained
    and flaked
1 egg, hard-boiled and chopped
    (optional)
30 ml (2 tbsp) chopped fresh
    parsley
10 ml (2 tsp) lemon juice
salt and pepper
1 egg, beaten
100 g (4 oz) dried breadcrumbs
30 ml (2 tbsp) vegetable oil
lemon wedges, to serve

1   Wash the potatoes thoroughly, but do not peel them. Prick them all over with a fork and microwave on HIGH for 8–10 minutes or until cooked.

2   Put the butter in a large bowl and microwave on HIGH for 45 seconds until melted. Stir in the onion and microwave on HIGH for 5–7 minutes until softened.

3   Cut the potatoes in half horizontally and scoop out the insides. Mash with the onion and butter. Stir in the tuna, egg (if using), parsley and lemon juice and season well with salt and pepper.

4   Preheat a browning dish to maximum according to the manufacturer's instructions.

5   Meanwhile, shape the potato mixture into 8 cakes and coat in the beaten egg and breadcrumbs seasoned with salt and pepper.

6   Add the oil to the browning dish then, without removing the dish from the oven, quickly add the fish cakes and microwave on HIGH for 2 minutes.

7   Turn the cakes over and microwave on HIGH for 2 minutes. Serve with lemon wedges.

BEEF BURGERS

MAKES 4

450 g (1 lb) lean minced beef
1 large onion, skinned and grated
5 ml (1 level tsp) salt
1.25 ml (¼ level tsp) cayenne pepper
30 ml (2 tbsp) vegetable oil
4 plain or toasted hamburger buns,
    to serve

1 Mix the beef and onion together and season with salt and cayenne pepper.

2 Divide the mixture into four and shape each piece into a neat burger about 2.5 cm (1 inch) thick.

3 Preheat a large browning dish to maximum according to the manufacturer's instructions, adding the oil for the last 30 seconds. (Alternatively, put the oil into a large shallow dish and microwave on HIGH for 1–2 minutes until hot.)

4 Without removing the dish from the oven, press two beef burgers flat on to the hot surface and microwave on HIGH for 2–3 minutes. Turn the burgers over, reposition them and microwave on HIGH for 2–3 minutes until cooked. Repeat with the remaining burgers.

As soon as the burgers are cooked serve them in plain or toasted hamburger buns.

CRISPY CHEESE
AND HAM SANDWICHES

MAKES 2 SANDWICHES

4 slices bread
10 ml (2 level tsp) Dijon mustard
2 slices cooked ham
50 g (2 oz) Cheddar cheese, grated
15 g (½ oz) butter or margarine

1 Preheat a browning dish to maximum according to the manufacturer's instructions.

2 Meanwhile, spread the bread with the mustard. Top two slices with the ham and then the cheese. Place the remaining slices of bread on top to make sandwiches.

3 Spread the butter on the outside of each sandwich.

4 As soon as the browning dish is ready and without removing the dish from the oven, put in the sandwiches. Microwave on HIGH for 15 seconds, then quickly turn the sandwiches over and microwave on HIGH for 15–20 seconds or until the cheese has almost settled.

5 Cut in half and serve immediately.

FRENCH BREAD PIZZA

SERVES 2

397 g (14 oz) can tomatoes,
    drained
15 ml (1 level tbsp) tomato purée
1 small onion, skinned and
    chopped
1 garlic clove, skinned and crushed
5 ml (1 level tsp) dried mixed herbs
salt and pepper
1 small French loaf
100 g (4 oz) Mozzarella or
    Cheddar cheese, grated
few olives and anchovy fillets
    (optional)

1 Put the tomatoes, tomato purée, onion, garlic, herbs and salt and pepper in a medium bowl and microwave on HIGH for 5 minutes or until hot and slightly reduced.

2 Cut the French bread in half horizontally then cut each length in half. Place crust side down, side by side, on a large flat serving plate.

3 Spoon the tomato topping on to the bread and cover with the grated cheese. Arrange the olives and anchovies, if using, on top of the cheese. Microwave on HIGH for 1 minute until heated through. Serve immediately.

PIGS IN BLANKETS

SERVES 4

4 slices of processed cheese
mustard or pickle
4 frankfurters
4 slices of streaky bacon, rinded

1 Spread the cheese slices with mustard or pickle and wrap them around the frankfurters. Wrap the bacon around the cheese.

2 Arrange in a circle on absorbent kitchen paper on a large plate or flat dish. Cover loosely with absorbent kitchen paper and microwave on HIGH for 4–5 minutes until the frankfurters are warm and the bacon is crisp, turning them over after 2 minutes. Remove the kitchen paper and serve.

WELSH RAREBIT

SERVES 2

25 g (1 oz) butter or margarine
5 ml (1 level tsp) mustard powder
pinch of salt
pinch of cayenne pepper
dash of Worcestershire sauce
75 g (3 oz) mature Cheddar cheese,
    grated
30 ml (2 tbsp) brown ale or milk
2 slices of bread, toasted

1 Put the butter in a medium bowl and microwave on HIGH for 20 seconds until softened.

2 Stir in the mustard, salt, cayenne pepper, Worcestershire sauce, grated cheese and ale or milk. Microwave on HIGH for about 30 seconds or until hot and bubbling.

3 Beat the cheese well then spread it over the toast. Place on serving plates and microwave on HIGH for 20–30 seconds until heated through. Serve immediately.

Variation

Onion Rarebit: Thinly slice one small onion and arrange on the bread before pouring the cheese mixture over.

DEVILLED CHICKEN LIVERS

SERVES 2

25 g (1 oz) butter or margarine
1 small onion, skinned and finely
    chopped
1 garlic clove, skinned and crushed
5 ml (1 level tsp) curry powder
100 g (4 oz) chicken livers,
    trimmed and cut into bite-sized
    pieces
pinch of cayenne pepper
salt and pepper
dash of Worcestershire sauce
10 ml (2 level tsp) tomato purée
4 thick slices of bread, toasted

1 Put the butter in a large shallow bowl and microwave on HIGH for 45 seconds until melted. Stir in the onion, garlic and curry powder and microwave on HIGH for 3–4 minutes or until slightly softened.

2 Stir in the chicken livers and cayenne pepper and season with salt and pepper. Stir in the Worcestershire sauce and tomato purée and 15–30 ml (1–2 tbsp) water to make a moist consistency.

3 Cover with cling film turned back slightly to allow steam to escape and microwave on HIGH for 3 minutes until the livers are just cooked, shaking the bowl occasionally.

4 Place the toast on two serving plates and spoon the chicken mixture over.

5 Microwave one plate at a time on HIGH for 30 seconds. Serve immediately.

POACHED EGGS

SERVES 2

2.5 ml (½ tsp) white vinegar
2 eggs
hot buttered toast, to serve

1 Pour 450 ml (¾ pint) boiling salted water and the vinegar into a large shallow dish and microwave on HIGH for 1–2 minutes until the water returns to the boil.

2 Carefully break each egg on to a saucer, prick the yolk with a fine skewer or needle and slide one at a time into the water.

3 Cover the dish with cling film and microwave on HIGH for 1 minute.

4 Pierce the cling film and leave the eggs to stand, covered, for 1–2 minutes to set. Using a slotted spoon, transfer the eggs to the hot buttered toast.

NOTE:

To poach 4 eggs, use 600 ml (1 pint) boiling salted water with 5 ml (1 tsp) vinegar and proceed as above. After adding the eggs, cover and cook for 1½–2 minutes.

SPAGHETTI CARBONARA

SERVES 4

225 g (8 oz) spaghetti
salt and pepper
2 eggs
100 g (4 oz) Cheddar cheese, finely
    grated
45 ml (3 level tbsp) freshly grated
    Parmesan cheese
225 g (8 oz) streaky bacon, rinded
    and chopped
150 ml ($\frac{1}{4}$ pint) double cream
chopped fresh parsley, to garnish
grated Parmesan cheese, to serve

1. Put the spaghetti in a 2.6 litre (4$\frac{1}{2}$-pint) bowl and pour 1.4 litres (2$\frac{1}{2}$ pints) boiling water over. Add salt to taste and stir once. Cover and microwave on HIGH for 7 minutes. Leave to stand, covered.

2. Meanwhile, beat the eggs and cheese together.

3. Place the bacon in a medium bowl, cover with absorbent kitchen paper, and microwave on HIGH for 5 minutes until slightly crisp.

4. Stir the cream into the bacon and season with salt and pepper. Microwave on HIGH for 2 minutes until heated through.

5. Drain the spaghetti well and tip into a warmed serving dish. Pour the egg and cheese mixture over and mix well. Stir in the bacon and cream mixture, sprinkle with parsley then Parmesan cheese. Serve at once.

SEAFOOD SALAD

SERVES 4

225 g (8 oz) firm white fish fillets,
    such as cod or haddock
100 g (4 oz) peeled prawns
$\frac{1}{2}$ small green pepper, finely diced
5 ml (1 tsp) lemon juice
120 ml (8 tbsp) mayonnaise
salt and pepper
shredded lettuce, to serve
black olives and paprika,
    to garnish

1. Place the fish on a plate and cover with cling film, pulling back one corner to allow the steam to escape.

2. Microwave on HIGH for about 3 minutes or until the flesh is just tender. If the fish is thick, turn it over after about 1$\frac{1}{2}$ minutes.

3. Leave the fish to stand, covered, until cool.

4. Cut the fish into cubes. Add the prawns and green pepper and mix together with the lemon juice and mayonnaise. Season with salt and pepper.

5. Line 4 scallop shells or individual dishes with shredded lettuce. Arrange fish mixture on top and garnish with olives and paprika.

SOUSED HERRINGS

SERVES 4
4 herrings, cleaned and boned
salt and pepper
150 ml (¼ pint) malt vinegar
3−4 black peppercorns
1 small onion, skinned and sliced
green salad, to serve

1 Trim the heads, tails and fins from the fish. Remove any remaining bones and sprinkle the inside of the fish with salt and pepper.

2 Roll the fish up, skin side out, from the head end. Secure with wooden cocktail sticks. Arrange in a single layer in a shallow dish.

3 Mix the vinegar with 150 ml (¼ pint) water, add the peppercorns and pour over the fish. Arrange the onion slices on top.

4 Cover with cling film, pulling back one corner to allow the steam to escape, and microwave on HIGH for 6−8 minutes, turning the dish after 3 minutes.

5 Leave the fish to cool in the liquid then chill. Serve with a green salad.

KIPPER PÂTÉ

SERVES 3−4
225 g (8 oz) frozen kipper fillets
75 g (3 oz) butter or margarine, diced
30 ml (2 tbsp) single cream
few drops anchovy essence
salt and pepper
hot buttered toast, to serve

1 Put the kippers in their wrapping on a plate. Cut a cross in the wrapping with a pair of scissors.

2 Microwave on LOW for about 8 minutes to thaw.

3 Put the butter into a small bowl. Microwave on HIGH for 45−60 seconds until melted.

4 Place the kippers in a blender or food processor with the cream, anchovy essence, pepper and a little salt and two thirds of the butter. Blend until smooth, switching the motor off and scraping down the sides of the goblet occasionally.

5 Turn the pâté into a small dish or individual ramekin dishes and cover with the remaining melted butter. Chill in the refrigerator. Serve with hot buttered toast.

EGG AND BACON

SERVES 1
2 slices of streaky bacon, rinded
1 egg

1 Snip the bacon fat at intervals. Place the bacon slices on a serving plate or in a shallow dish and cover with absorbent kitchen paper.

2 Microwave on HIGH for 1–1½ minutes, depending on the thickness of the bacon.

3 Remove from the plate or dish and add the egg. Prick the egg yolk with a fine skewer or needle and cover with cling film.

4 Microwave on HIGH for about 30 seconds then leave to stand, covered, for 1 minute.

5 Return the bacon to the plate or dish and cook, covered, for 15–30 seconds.

WALNUT SPREAD OR DIP

SERVES ABOUT 6
15 g (½ oz) butter or margarine
225 g (8 oz) cream cheese
150 ml (¼ pint) natural yogurt
½ medium green pepper, chopped
¼ small red pepper, chopped
5 ml (1 level tsp) garlic salt
pinch of pepper
100 g (4 oz) walnuts, chopped
paprika, to garnish

1 Put the butter in a small bowl and microwave on HIGH for 30 seconds until melted.

2 Put the cream cheese in a medium bowl and microwave on HIGH for 30–45 seconds to soften. Add the melted butter and yogurt and beat until smooth.

3 Stir in the green and red pepper, garlic salt, pepper and most of the walnuts. Mix well.

4 Turn the mixture into a serving dish and refrigerate until thickened. Sprinkle with paprika and the remaining walnuts.

Serves as a spread on small savoury biscuits or as a dip, accompanied by raw vegetables, such as carrot sticks, cauliflower florets and radishes, and Melba toast.

MAIN COURSES

MEAT AND POULTRY DISHES

Meat and poultry cooked in a microwave oven remain moist and juicy. Small cuts and joints that cook in less than 15–20 minutes can easily be given an attractive colour (see page 20). Boned and rolled meat and poultry cook more evenly because the shape and thickness are consistent. If the bone is left in, cover the thin area of flesh over the bone with aluminium foil for the first half of the cooking. Also, position the piece of meat so the thickest parts are pointing towards the edge of the dish. Tie boned joints or cuts in a neat shape with string, and if a stuffing is included, add extra time to the cooking. Turn large joints or cuts over at least once during cooking and as they need 15–20 minutes standing time, cover them with aluminium foil and leave in a warm place.

FISH DISHES

The cooking time for fish is so short that it retains its juices, texture and shape – and the house-pervading smell is minimal. But remember that the flesh will continue to cook after the oven has been switched off, so take care not to let it overcook. This is particularly critical with shellfish. Slash the skin of whole fish in one or two places and arrange the fish with the thinnest parts towards the centre of the cooker. If cooking more than one fish, overlap the thin parts, keeping them separate with a small piece of cling film or foil. Fillets may be rolled up but large fish should be cooked in a single layer. All fish with the exception of breadcrumbed pieces, should be covered with pierced cling film.

RICE AND PASTA DISHES

Boil the water in a kettle then place it in a large bowl with the rice or pasta. Stir once during cooking and remove the rice or pasta from the cooker when it is still slightly undercooked and allow it to finish cooking during the standing time.

SPICY PORK CHOPS

SERVES 4

4 pork spare rib back chops
1 garlic clove, skinned and crushed
1 small onion, skinned and finely
    chopped
15 ml (1 level tbsp) cornflour
150 ml (¼ pint) natural yogurt
15 ml (1 level tbsp) tomato purée
5 ml (1 level tsp) ground turmeric
5 ml (1 level tsp) paprika
2.5 ml (½ level tsp) chilli powder
salt and pepper

1 Trim off any excess fat from the chops and arrange them in a single layer in a round shallow dish. Prick all over with a fork.

2 Mix all the remaining ingredients together and spread over both sides of the chops. Cover and leave to marinate for at least 4 hours, preferably overnight.

3 Cover with cling film, pulling back one corner to allow the steam to escape. Microwave on HIGH for 5 minutes. Turn the chops over, reposition, re-cover and microwave on HIGH for 10–12 minutes until tender. Leave to stand, covered, for 5 minutes.

STUFFED PEPPERS

SERVES 4

4 green or red peppers
1 small onion, skinned and
    chopped
1 garlic clove, skinned and chopped
15 ml (1 tbsp) vegetable oil
15 ml (1 level tbsp) medium curry
    powder
225 g (8 oz) lean minced beef
50 g (2 oz) long grain white rice
150 ml ($\frac{1}{4}$ pint) boiling beef stock
salt and pepper
150 ml ($\frac{1}{4}$ pint) natural yogurt

1 Cut a slice from the top of each pepper and remove the cores and seeds. Stand the peppers with the slices cut from the tops, in a shallow dish that they just fit. Add 60 ml (4 tbsp) water. Three-quarters cover with cling film and microwave on HIGH for 6 minutes. If the oven does not have a turn-table, quarter turn the dish three times during cooking. Leave to stand.

2 Mix the onion, garlic, oil and curry powder together in a large bowl and microwave on HIGH for 5 minutes, stirring occasionally.

3 Stir in the beef, rice and stock and microwave on HIGH for 8 minutes, or until the rice is tender and most of the liquid has been absorbed, stirring occasionally. Stir in the yogurt and mix well. Season with salt and pepper.

4 Fill the peppers with the meat mixture and cover with the slices of pepper. Cover and microwave on LOW for 10 minutes or until the peppers are tender and the filling is hot. If the oven is not fitted with a turntable, quarter turn the dish three times during cooking.

CAULIFLOWER CHEESE

SERVES 4

1 cauliflower, prepared weight
    about 700 g (1$\frac{1}{2}$ lb), broken into
    florets
25 g (1 oz) butter or margarine
25 g (1 oz) plain flour
300 ml ($\frac{1}{2}$ pint) milk
pinch of mustard powder
salt and pepper
75 g (3 oz) Cheddar cheese, grated

1 Place the prepared cauliflower in a large bowl with 60 ml (4 tbsp) water.

2 Three-quarters cover with cling film and microwave on HIGH for 10–12 minutes until just tender. Drain and place in a 1.1 litre (2 pint) serving dish.

3 Put the butter, flour, milk, mustard, salt and pepper in a medium bowl and blend well.

4 Microwave on HIGH for about 4 minutes until the sauce has boiled and thickened, whisking every minute.

5 Whisk until smooth then stir in the grated cheese and pour over the cauliflower.

6 Microwave on HIGH for 3–5 minutes until heated through.

7 Leave to stand for 2–3 minutes before serving.

CHICKEN MEAT LOAF

SERVES 6

225 g (8 oz) streaky bacon rashers,
    rinded
25 g (1 oz) butter or margarine
1 small onion, skinned and finely
    chopped
2 garlic cloves, skinned and
    crushed
225 g (8 oz) chicken breast fillet,
    skinned and finely chopped
225 g (8 oz) lean pork, finely
    chopped
175 g (6 oz) chicken livers, finely
    chopped
15 ml (1 tbsp) brandy
1 egg, beaten
salt and pepper
5 ml (1 level tsp) dried thyme
60 ml (4 tbsp) double cream
French bread and a salad, to serve

1. Stretch the bacon with the back of a knife and use it to line a 700 g (1½ lb) non-metallic loaf dish, reserving a few slices.

2. Put the butter in a large bowl and microwave on HIGH for 30 seconds until melted.

3. Add the onion and garlic and three-quarters cover with cling film or a lid. Microwave on HIGH for 5–7 minutes until soft, stirring occasionally.

4. Add the chicken, pork and chicken livers to the onion mixture with the remaining ingredients. Mix together well.

5. Spread the mixture into the loaf dish taking care not to disturb the bacon. Fold the ends of the bacon over the mixture. Cover with the reserved bacon and then loosely cover with greaseproof paper.

6. Microwave on HIGH for 25 minutes until the juices run clear when a wooden cocktail stick is inserted in the centre. Remove the greaseproof paper after 15 minutes and, if the oven does not have a turntable, give the dish a quarter turn three times during cooking.

7. When cooked, place a plate on top of the meat loaf and weight it down. Allow it to cool, then chill it overnight.

8. Serve cut into slices with French bread and a salad.

POACHED FISH

SERVES 4

700 g (1½ lb) white fish fillets or
    cutlets
salt and pepper
50 ml (2 fl oz) milk
15 g (½ oz) butter or margarine

1. Place the fish in a single layer in a shallow dish.

2. Mix the seasoning with the milk and pour over the fish. Flake the butter on top.

3. Cover the dish with cling film, pulling back one corner to allow the steam to escape, and microwave on HIGH for 5–6 minutes or until the fish flakes when tested with a fork. Leave to stand, covered, for 5 minutes before serving.

CHILLI CON CARNE

SERVES 6

1 large onion, skinned and chopped
1 green pepper, seeded and cut into
    strips
15 ml (1 tbsp) vegetable oil
700 g (1½ lb) lean minced beef
397 g (14 oz) can chopped
    tomatoes
30 ml (2 level tbsp) tomato purée
15 ml (1 tbsp) red wine vinegar
5 ml (1 level tsp) soft dark brown
    sugar
5–10 ml (1–2 level tsp) chilli
    powder
15 ml (1 level tbsp) ground cumin
salt and pepper
439 g (15½ oz) can red kidney
    beans, drained and rinsed
cooked rice (see page 91)
    and a green salad, to serve

1 Put the onion, pepper and oil in a large bowl and mix together. Microwave on HIGH for 5 minutes or until softened, stirring once. Add the beef, breaking up any large pieces. Microwave on HIGH for 6–8 minutes or until the meat starts to change colour, stirring after 3 minutes.

2 Mix together the tomatoes, tomato purée, vinegar, sugar, chilli powder and cumin. Season with salt and pepper then stir into the meat. Cover with cling film and microwave on HIGH for 30 minutes, stirring once halfway through.

3 Stir in the beans, re-cover the dish and microwave on HIGH for 5 minutes.
Serve with cooked rice and a green salad.

HADDOCK AND SPINACH PIE

SERVES 4

50 g (2 oz) butter or margarine
50 g (2 oz) plain flour
450 ml (¾ pint) milk
100 g (4 oz) Cheddar cheese,
    grated
salt and pepper
freshly grated nutmeg
454 g (1 lb) packet frozen leaf
    spinach
450 g (1 lb) smoked haddock fillet,
    skinned and cut into 2.5 cm
    (1 inch) strips
boiled or creamed potatoes, to serve

1 Blend the butter, flour and milk together in a large bowl and microwave on HIGH for 4–5 minutes until the sauce has thickened, whisking after every minute.

2 Stir in half of the cheese and season well with salt, pepper and nutmeg. Set aside.

3 Put the frozen spinach in a deep 20.5 cm (8 inch) square dish and microwave on HIGH for 6–7 minutes until thawed.

4 Turn into a sieve and drain thoroughly, then spread evenly over the base of the dish.

5 Place the fish in a single layer on top of the spinach and microwave on HIGH for 4–5 minutes or until tender and the flesh flakes easily.

6 Pour the cheese sauce evenly over the fish to cover it completely. Microwave on HIGH for 5 minutes, then sprinkle the remaining cheese on top.

7 Brown under a hot grill, if desired. Serve with boiled or creamed potatoes.

CHICKEN CURRY

SERVES 4

15 g (½ oz) butter or margarine
1 medium onion, skinned and
    finely chopped
4 chicken quarters, skinned and
    halved
30 ml (2 level tbsp) medium curry
    powder
15 ml (1 level tbsp) plain flour
600 ml (1 pint) chicken stock
5 ml (1 tsp) Worcestershire sauce
15 ml (1 level tbsp) tomato purée
15 ml (1 tbsp) lemon juice
30 ml (2 level tbsp) mango chutney
50 g (2 oz) sultanas
1 dessert apple, peeled, cored and
    chopped
salt and pepper
cooked rice (see page 91), to serve

1 Put the butter and onion in a large round casserole. Add the chicken, placing the thinnest parts towards the centre. Microwave on HIGH for 10–12 minutes until the chicken is tender, turning the quarters over once. Remove the chicken from the dish and set aside.

2 Stir the curry powder and flour into the casserole and microwave on HIGH for 30 seconds.

3 Gradually blend in the stock. Microwave on HIGH for 4 minutes, stirring occasionally, until the sauce has thickened.

4 Stir in the Worcestershire sauce, tomato purée, lemon juice, chutney, sultanas, apple and season with salt and pepper. Return the chicken to the casserole.

5 Cover and microwave on HIGH for 8 minutes until heated through.

6 Leave to stand, covered, for 5 minutes. Serve with cooked rice.

COD STEAKS WITH PRAWNS AND CREAM

SERVES 4

40 g (1½ oz) butter or margarine
1 medium onion, skinned and
    chopped
40 g (1½ oz) plain flour
300 ml (½ pint) milk
150 ml (¼ pint) single cream
5 ml (1 level tsp) prepared mustard
100 g (4 oz) peeled prawns
10 ml (2 tsp) lemon juice
salt and pepper
4 cod steaks, each weighing about
    175 g (6 oz)
chopped fresh parsley, to garnish

1 Put the butter in a large bowl and microwave on HIGH for 45 seconds until melted.

2 Stir in the onion and three-quarters cover with cling film or a lid. Microwave on HIGH for 5–7 minutes, stirring occasionally until softened.

3 Stir in the flour, then the milk and microwave on HIGH for 2–3 minutes until thickened, whisking after every minute.

4 Stir in the cream, mustard, prawns and lemon juice and season well with salt and pepper.

5 Arrange the cod in a single layer in a round serving dish, with the thinnest parts of the fish towards the centre. Pour the sauce over and microwave on HIGH for 4 minutes per 450 g (1 lb) turning once, until the fish is tender and flakes when tested with a fork. Garnish with chopped parsley.

CHICKEN BREASTS CORDON BLEU

SERVES 4

4 chicken breasts, skinned and
    boned
40 g (1½ oz) butter or margarine
salt and pepper
4 thin slices ham
4 thin slices Mozzarella cheese
15 ml (1 tbsp) grated Parmesan
    cheese
paprika

1 Place the chicken breasts between two pieces of greaseproof paper or cling film and beat them with a meat bat or rolling pin until flattened.

2 Put the butter in a shallow dish large enough to hold the chicken breasts in a single layer and microwave on HIGH for 45 seconds until melted.

3 Add the chicken breasts, turning them to coat with the melted butter.

4 Cover with cling film, pulling back one corner to allow the steam to escape, and cook on HIGH for 15–20 minutes or until tender. If the oven does not have a turntable, turn the dish after 10 minutes.

5 Drain the chicken and reserve the juices. Season the chicken breasts with salt and pepper.

6 Top each breast with a slice of ham and then a slice of cheese. Brush with the reserved juices and sprinkle Parmesan cheese and paprika over.

7 Cover and microwave on HIGH for about 3 minutes or until the cheese just melts.

PORK AND VEGETABLES

SERVES 4

30 ml (2 tbsp) vegetable oil
60 ml (4 tbsp) soy sauce
15 ml (1 tbsp) dry sherry
12.5 ml (2½ level tsp) cornflour
6.25 ml (1¼ level tsp) sugar
2.5 ml (½ tsp) finely chopped fresh
    ginger or 1.25 ml (¼ level tsp)
    ground ginger
1 garlic clove, skinned and crushed
450 g (1 lb) pork fillet, cut into
    matchstick strips
2 large carrots, peeled and cut into
    matchstick strips
1 green pepper, cut into thin strips
3 spring onions, cut into 2.5 cm
    (1 inch) lengths
225 g (8 oz) mushrooms, sliced
cooked rice (see page 91), to serve

1 Stir the oil, soy sauce, sherry, cornflour, sugar, ginger and garlic together in a medium casserole. Add the pork, mix well and leave to marinate for at least 30 minutes.

2 Stir in the remaining ingredients and microwave on HIGH for 7–8 minutes until the pork is tender and the juices run clear and the vegetables are tender but still firm, stirring occasionally.

Serve with cooked rice.

SALMON STEAKS WITH HOLLANDAISE SAUCE

SERVES 4

4 salmon steaks, cut 4 cm
    (1½ inches) thick and weighing
    about 175 g (6 oz) each
15 ml (1 tbsp) lemon juice
salt
Hollandaise Sauce
100 g (4 oz) butter, diced
30 ml (2 tbsp) lemon juice or
    white wine vinegar
2 egg yolks
salt and pepper

1. Arrange the steaks in a single layer in a shallow dish with the thickest part of the flesh towards the outside of the dish.

2. Mix 150 ml (¼ pint) water, the lemon juice and salt together and pour over the fish.

3. Cover the dish with cling film, pulling back one corner to allow the steam to escape, and microwave on HIGH for 6–8 minutes or until the water just comes to the boil. Turn the dish twice during cooking if the oven does not have a turntable.

4. If serving hot, leave the dish to stand for 5 minutes. If serving cold, leave to cool in the liquid, then chill.

5. To make the sauce, put the butter into a medium bowl and microwave on HIGH for 1–1½ minutes until melted.

6. Remove from the oven and whisk in the lemon juice or wine vinegar and the egg yolks.

7. Return to the oven and microwave on HIGH for 30–45 seconds or until just thick enough to coat the back of a spoon, stirring briskly every 15 seconds. Season with salt and pepper, pour over the salmon and serve.

BOEUF BOURGUIGNONNE

SERVES 4

100 g (4 oz) streaky bacon, rinded
    and chopped
700 g (1½ lb) sirloin steak, trimmed
    and cut into 2.5 cm (1 inch)
    cubes
1 garlic clove, skinned and chopped
175 g (6 oz) silverskin or baby
    onions, skinned and left whole
100 g (4 oz) button mushrooms
5 ml (1 level tsp) dried mixed herbs
salt and pepper
15 ml (1 tbsp) plain flour
225 ml (8 fl oz) red wine
chopped fresh parsley, to garnish

1. Put the chopped bacon in a large casserole and microwave on HIGH for 3 minutes.

2. Add the steak, garlic, onions, mushrooms, herbs and seasoning and mix together. Sprinkle over the flour and stir in. Microwave on HIGH for 1 minute, then gradually stir in the red wine.

3. Three-quarters cover with cling film or a lid and microwave on HIGH for 5 minutes until boiling. Reduce to LOW and cook for 40–50 minutes until the meat is tender, stirring occasionally.

Serve garnished with chopped parsley.

FISH WITH MIXED VEGETABLES

SERVES 4–6

226 g (8 oz) packet frozen cut green
    beans
15 ml (1 tbsp) vegetable oil
2 medium carrots, thinly sliced
1 celery stalk, finely sliced
1 medium onion, skinned and
    finely chopped
397 g (14 oz) can chopped
    tomatoes
1 bay leaf
pinch of dried thyme
salt and pepper
900 g (2 lb) firm white fish fillet,
    such as cod or haddock, skinned
    and cut into 5 cm (2 inch) cubes

1   Slit the bag of green beans open and place on a plate or in a dish. Microwave on HIGH for 6 minutes, shaking the bag occasionally during cooking.

2   Put the oil, carrot, celery and onion in a large shallow dish and cover with a lid or cling film, pulling back one corner to allow the steam to escape. Microwave on HIGH for 8–10 minutes, stirring occasionally, until the vegetables are softened.

3   Stir in the tomatoes and their juice, the bay leaf and thyme and season with salt and pepper. Microwave on HIGH for 5 minutes or until boiling.

4   Stir in the fish and microwave on HIGH for 8 minutes, stirring occasionally. Drain the cooked beans and stir into the fish. Microwave on HIGH for 2 minutes until the fish is tender and flakes when tested with a fork.

CHICKEN WITH TOMATO AND PAPRIKA

SERVES 4

30 ml (2 tbsp) vegetable oil
1 medium onion, skinned and
    finely chopped
450 g (1 lb) chicken breast fillet,
    skinned and cut into 2.5 cm
    (1 inch) strips
30 ml (2 level tbsp) paprika
1.25 ml ($\frac{1}{4}$ level tsp) chilli
    seasoning
225 ml (8 fl oz) tomato juice
salt and pepper
30 ml (2 level tbsp) cornflour
100 ml (4 fl oz) soured cream
chopped fresh parsley, to garnish
cooked rice (see page 91), to serve

1   Put the oil and onion in a large bowl and three-quarters cover with cling film or a lid. Microwave on HIGH for 5–7 minutes until softened, stirring occasionally.

2   Add the chicken, paprika and chilli seasoning and mix well together. Gradually stir in the tomato juice and season with salt and pepper.

3   Blend the cornflour to a smooth paste with about 45 ml (3 tbsp) water, then stir into the bowl.

4   Microwave on HIGH for 6–7 minutes or until the chicken is tender and the sauce is bubbling and thickened, stirring frequently.

5   Gradually stir in the soured cream and microwave on MEDIUM for 1 minute or until heated through but not boiling. Garnish with chopped parsley.

    Serve with cooked rice.

LASAGNE

SERVES 4

175 g (6 oz) lasagne
45 ml (3 tbsp) vegetable oil
salt and pepper
1 medium onion, skinned and
  finely chopped
450 g (1 lb) lean minced beef
30 ml (2 level tbsp) plain flour
10 ml (2 level tsp) dried basil,
  chopped
397 g (14 oz) can chopped
  tomatoes
150 ml (¼ pint) hot beef stock
175 g (6 oz) mushrooms, wiped
  and sliced
300 ml (½ pint) white sauce (see
  page 79)
100 g (4 oz) Cheddar cheese,
  grated
green salad, to serve

1 Place the lasagne in a 5 cm (2 inch) deep rectangular casserole. Spoon 5 ml (1 tsp) oil over and add 900 ml (1½ pints) boiling water and a pinch of salt. Cover with the casserole lid or cling film and microwave on HIGH for 9 minutes. Leave to stand for 15 minutes, then drain well and rinse.

2 Mix the remaining oil and the onion in a medium bowl. Microwave on HIGH for 3 minutes, stirring once. Add the meat, breaking up any large pieces, and microwave on HIGH for 5 minutes, stirring once.

3 Sprinkle the flour over, then stir in with the basil, tomatoes, stock and mushrooms. Season with salt and pepper. Microwave on HIGH for 20 minutes, stirring once.

4 Layer the lasagne and meat sauce in the casserole dish, finishing with a layer of sauce. Pour the white sauce over and microwave on HIGH for 2 minutes or until heated through.

5 Sprinkle the cheese over, and place under a hot grill until the cheese is bubbling and has melted. Serve with a green salad.

CHICKEN VERONIQUE

SERVES 4

50 g (2 oz) butter or margarine
50 g (2 oz) plain flour
300 ml (½ pint) chicken stock
300 ml (½ pint) dry white wine
450 g (1 lb) cooked chicken or
  turkey meat, cut into 5 cm
  (2 inch) pieces
150 ml (¼ pint) single cream
100 g (4 oz) seedless green grapes
salt and pepper
cooked rice (see page 91), to serve

1 Put the butter in a large bowl and microwave on HIGH for 45 seconds or until melted.

2 Blend in the flour and microwave on HIGH for 30 seconds. Gradually stir in the stock and wine.

3 Microwave on HIGH for 3–5 minutes until the sauce has thickened, stirring once or twice to prevent lumps forming.

4 Stir in the cooked chicken or turkey meat, cream and grapes and season with salt and pepper.

5 Cover with cling film and microwave on LOW for 4–5 minutes until heated through. DO NOT ALLOW TO BOIL.

6 Leave to stand, covered, for 5 minutes. Serve with cooked rice.

CHICKEN RISOTTO

SERVES 4

2 chicken leg portions
30 ml (2 tbsp) vegetable oil
1 large onion, skinned and chopped
100 g (4 oz) mushrooms, sliced
1 green pepper, seeded and sliced
900 ml (1½ pints) boiling chicken
  stock
450 g (1 lb) long grain white rice
salt and pepper
30 ml (2 level tbsp) chopped fresh
  parsley
green salad, to serve

1 Put the chicken and oil in a large casserole dish with the thinnest part of the portions towards the centre. Microwave on HIGH for 6–7 minutes, until cooked, turning them over halfway through the cooking. Remove from the dish and set aside to cool.

2 Stir the onion and vegetables into the oil remaining in the casserole dish and microwave on HIGH for 5–7 minutes or until softened, stirring once.

3 Cut the chicken meat into bite-sized pieces, discarding the skin and bones, and add to the casserole with the stock and rice. Season with salt and pepper. Mix well, cover and microwave on HIGH for 13 minutes.

4 Leave to stand, covered, for 10 minutes. Mix lightly with a fork and stir in the chopped parsley.
  Serve with a green salad.

VEGETABLE HOTPOT

SERVES 4–6

450 g (1 lb) potatoes, peeled and
  very thinly sliced
450 g (1 lb) carrots, peeled and
  very thinly sliced
2 leeks, trimmed and thinly sliced
2 celery sticks, thinly sliced
1 large onion, skinned and thinly
  sliced
1.25 ml (¼ level tsp) dried thyme
1 bay leaf
300 ml (½ pint) boiling chicken
  stock
10 ml (2 level tsp) tomato purée
salt and pepper
432 g (15 oz) can red kidney beans,
  drained and rinsed
50 g (2 oz) butter or margarine
75 g (3 oz) fresh breadcrumbs
75 g (3 oz) rolled oats
175 g (6 oz) Cheddar cheese,
  grated

1 Put the potatoes, carrots, leeks, celery, onion, thyme and bay leaf in a large casserole and mix thoroughly.

2 Blend the chicken stock and tomato purée together, pour over the vegetables and season well with salt and pepper.

3 Three-quarters cover with a lid or cling film and microwave on HIGH for 15–20 minutes until the vegetables are tender, stirring occasionally. Stir in the kidney beans and set aside.

4 Put the butter in a shallow dish and microwave on HIGH for 45 seconds until melted.

5 Stir in the breadcrumbs and oats and mix well together. Microwave on HIGH for 1–2 minutes or until the breadcrumbs and oats are slightly brown. Stir in the cheese.

6 Spoon the cheese mixture evenly over the vegetables and microwave on HIGH for 2 minutes or until hot. Brown under a hot grill, if desired.

PORK SUPRÊME

SERVES 4

225 g (8 oz) carrots, peeled and
  sliced
3 celery sticks, trimmed and thinly
  sliced
15 ml (1 tbsp) vegetable oil
4 boneless pork chops, trimmed
15 ml (1 level tbsp) prepared
  mustard
300 ml (½ pint) onion sauce (see
  page 79)
450 g (1 lb) potatoes, peeled and
  thinly sliced
15 g (½ oz) butter, softened

1 Mix the carrots, celery and oil together in a large shallow casserole. Microwave on HIGH for 5–7 minutes until softened, stirring once.

2 Arrange the chops in a single layer on the vegetables.

3 Mix the mustard into the onion sauce and pour over the chops.

4 Arrange the potato slices on top. Three-quarters cover with the casserole lid or cling film and microwave on HIGH for 30 minutes until the meat is tender.

5 Spread the butter over the potatoes and place under a hot grill until golden brown.

ITALIAN MEATBALLS

SERVES 4

450 g (1 lb) lean minced beef
25 g (1 oz) fresh breadcrumbs
1 small onion, skinned and finely
  chopped
25 g (1 oz) grated Parmesan cheese
salt and pepper
1 egg, beaten
425 g (15 oz) can tomato juice
5 ml (1 tsp) chopped fresh parsley
½ small green pepper, finely
  chopped
½ small red pepper, finely chopped
cooked spaghetti (see page 91),
  to serve

1 Mix together the minced beef, breadcrumbs, onion, cheese, and salt and pepper. Bind together with the beaten egg.

2 With wet hands, shape the mixture into 20 small meatballs and place them in a large casserole.

3 Three-quarters cover with cling film or a lid and microwave on HIGH for 5–7 minutes, turning the meatballs over after 3 minutes.

4 Mix together the tomato juice, chopped parsley, peppers and salt and pepper. Pour over the meatballs.

5 Recover and microwave on HIGH for 8–10 minutes, or until the meatballs are cooked. Stir gently after every 4 minutes.

Serve with cooked spaghetti.

VEGETABLE MOUSSAKA

SERVES 4–6

2 large aubergines, cut into 0.5 cm
($\frac{1}{4}$ inch) slices
salt and pepper
15 ml (1 tbsp) vegetable oil
1 large onion, skinned and chopped
2 garlic cloves, skinned and
  crushed
397 g (14 oz) can tomatoes
15 ml (1 level tbsp) tomato purée
5 ml (1 level tsp) sugar
5 ml (1 level tsp) dried basil
450 g (1 lb) courgettes, roughly
  chopped
150 ml ($\frac{1}{4}$ pint) natural yogurt
5 ml (1 level tsp) cornflour
100 g (4 oz) Cheddar cheese,
  grated

1 Put the aubergines into a colander, sprinkle with salt and leave for about 30 minutes to extract any bitter juices. Rinse in cold, running water and dry thoroughly with absorbent kitchen paper.

2 Put the oil, onion, garlic, tomatoes and their juice, tomato purée, sugar, basil and courgettes in a large bowl and microwave on HIGH for 12–15 minutes or until the courgettes are softened and the liquid has slightly reduced. Season well with salt and pepper.

3 Spread half of the tomato mixture in the bottom of a shallow flameproof dish.

4 Arrange half of the aubergine slices in a single layer on top of the tomato mixture. Repeat the layers ending with a layer of aubergines.

5 Microwave on HIGH for 10 minutes or until the aubergine is tender.

6 Meanwhile, blend the yogurt into the cornflour then stir in the cheese and season well with salt and pepper.

7 Spread the yogurt mixture in an even layer on top of the moussaka and microwave for a further 1–2 minutes or until hot. Brown under a hot grill, if desired.

8 Leave to stand for 5 minutes.

LIVER WITH SAGE AND ONIONS

SERVES 4

45 ml (3 tbsp) vegetable oil
2 large onions, skinned and thinly
  sliced
5 ml (1 level tsp) dried chopped
  sage
450 g (1 lb) lamb's liver, trimmed
  and cut into small, thin strips
30 ml (2 level tbsp) plain flour
300 ml ($\frac{1}{2}$ pint) chicken stock
salt and pepper

1 In a large shallow dish, mix the oil, onions and sage together and microwave on HIGH for 5–7 minutes, stirring frequently, until the onion has softened.

2 Add the liver to the dish. Sprinkle the flour over, stir the ingredients together then microwave on HIGH for 30 seconds. Gradually stir in the stock and salt and pepper and microwave on HIGH for 5–7 minutes until the liver is tender.

LAMB WITH MINT AND YOGURT

SERVES 4

15 ml (1 tbsp) vegetable oil

1 medium onion, skinned and
    sliced

3 bay leaves

75 ml (5 tbsp) white wine vinegar

salt and pepper

1.25 kg (2¾ lb) leg of lamb, boned
    and cut into 2.5 cm (1 inch)
    cubes

15 ml (1 level tbsp) cornflour

5 ml (1 level tsp) granulated sugar

150 ml (¼ pint) natural yogurt

45 ml (3 level tbsp) chopped fresh
    mint

30 ml (2 level tbsp) chopped fresh
    parsley

cooked noodles or rice, to serve

1 Put the oil, onion, bay leaves, vinegar and salt and pepper in a large casserole. Microwave on HIGH for 5 minutes until bubbling. Stir the lamb into the casserole, three-quarters cover with the casserole lid or cling film and microwave on MEDIUM for 30 minutes until the meat is tender giving the dish a quarter turn four times during cooking if the oven is not fitted with a turntable. Leave to stand, covered, for 5 minutes.

2 Meanwhile, in a small bowl mix the cornflour and sugar to a smooth paste with 15 ml (1 tbsp) water. Stir into the casserole then microwave on HIGH for 3 minutes, stirring after each minute, until thickened. Stir in the yogurt, mint and parsley and season with salt and pepper.

Serve with cooked noodles or rice.

MACARONI WITH CHEESE
AND GREEN PEPPER

SERVES 2–3

50 g (2 oz) butter or margarine,
    diced

1 small onion, skinned and finely
    chopped

½ green pepper, seeded and finely
    chopped

5 ml (1 level tsp) prepared mustard

salt and pepper

225 g (8 oz) short cut macaroni

225 g (8 oz) Cheddar cheese,
    grated

10 stuffed green olives, sliced
    (optional)

1 Put the butter in a large bowl and microwave on HIGH for 45 seconds until melted. Stir in the onion and green pepper and three-quarters cover with cling film or a lid. Microwave on HIGH for 5–7 minutes until softened, stirring occasionally.

2 Stir in the mustard, salt and pepper and macaroni and mix together well. Pour 450 ml (¾ pint) boiling water over, cover and microwave on HIGH for 7 minutes.

3 Stir in the cheese and the olives, if using, and leave to stand, covered, for 5 minutes.

VEGETABLES

Not only are the flavours of vegetables enhanced when cooked in a microwave cooker but their texture, shape, fresh colour and nutritional value are preserved. With the exception of vegetables with skins, such as potatoes which should be pricked to prevent them exploding, cover fresh vegetables with cling film and use the minimum of water or butter (about 15–30 ml (1–2 tbsp)) to create steam for cooking. However, vegetables such as mushrooms and spinach need no additional liquid and nor do frozen vegetables.

Cut root vegetables into small even-sized pieces to ensure they cook evenly. Arrange vegetables, such as cauliflower and broccoli sprigs, with the thickest part pointing towards the edge of the dish.

Small portions of vegetables (up to a weight of 450 g (1 lb)) make the most effective use of the oven. If cooking vegetables on their own, do not add salt directly to them until after they have been cooked.

RUNNER BEANS WITH TOMATO AND ONION

SERVES 4–6

15 ml (1 tbsp) vegetable oil
1 medium onion, skinned and
    finely chopped
1 garlic clove, skinned and crushed
5 large tomatoes, skinned and
    chopped
15 ml (1 tbsp) chopped fresh basil
    or parsley
salt and pepper
700 g (1½ lb) runner beans, topped
    and tailed and cut into 2.5 cm
    (1 inch) lengths
chopped fresh basil or parsley,
    to garnish

1 | Put the oil in a large bowl with the onion and garlic and microwave on HIGH for 5–7 minutes until softened.

2 | Stir in the tomatoes, basil or parsley, salt and pepper and microwave on HIGH for 5 minutes, stirring occasionally, to make a thick purée.

3 | Add the beans to the tomato mixture, cover with cling film, pulling back one corner to allow the steam to escape, and microwave on HIGH for 12–15 minutes or until the beans are just tender, stirring occasionally. Serve sprinkled with basil or parsley.

RATATOUILLE

SERVES 4

2 medium aubergines, cut into
  5 cm (2 inch) slices
salt and pepper
30 ml (2 tbsp) vegetable oil
4 tomatoes, skinned and sliced
1 small green pepper, seeded and
  chopped
2 medium onions, skinned and
  sliced
2 medium courgettes, cut into 1 cm
  (½ inch) slices
1 garlic clove, skinned and crushed
  (optional)

1 Put the aubergine slices into a colander or sieve, sprinkle both sides with salt and leave to stand for 30 minutes. Rinse in cold running water and dry well with absorbent kitchen paper.

2 Put the oil in a large casserole dish or bowl and add the vegetables, salt and pepper and garlic. Stir well, cover with a lid or cling film, pulling back one corner to allow the steam to escape.

3 Microwave on HIGH for 15–20 minutes until the vegetables are tender, stirring occasionally. Leave to stand, covered, for 5 minutes.

BROCCOLI WITH LEMON

SERVES 4

15 ml (1 tbsp) vegetable oil
1 small onion, skinned and finely
  chopped
1 garlic clove, skinned and crushed
  (optional)
700 g (1½ lb) broccoli florets,
  divided into small florets
grated rind and juice of 1 lemon
salt and pepper

1 Put the oil in a large bowl and add the onion and garlic, if using. Cover with cling film, pulling back a corner to allow the steam to escape, and microwave on HIGH for 5–7 minutes or until softened.

2 Add the broccoli and the lemon rind and juice.

3 Re-cover and microwave on HIGH for 7–10 minutes until the broccoli is just tender, stirring occasionally. Season with salt and pepper.

CARROT MAYONNAISE

SERVES 4

450 g (1 lb) new carrots, trimmed
  and scrubbed
5 ml (1 level tsp) French mustard
5 ml (1 tsp) lemon juice
45 ml (3 tbsp) single cream
30 ml (2 tbsp) chopped fresh chives
salt and pepper
150 ml (¼ pint) mayonnaise

1 Cut the carrots into 4 cm (1½ inch) lengths, then cut into quarters length ways.

2 Put the carrots into a large bowl with 30 ml (2 tbsp) water. Cover with cling film, pulling back one corner to allow the steam to escape. Microwave on HIGH for 6–8 minutes, stirring occasionally.

3 Drain, rinse in cold running water then drain well.

4 Stir the mustard, lemon juice, cream, chives, salt and pepper into the mayonnaise then carefully stir in the carrots. Chill for 1–2 hours before serving.

SPICY CAULIFLOWER WITH YOGURT

SERVES 4–6
30 ml (2 tbsp) vegetable oil
5 ml (1 level tsp) medium curry
    powder
2.5 ml (½ level tsp) mustard powder
2.5 ml (½ level tsp) turmeric
pinch of cayenne pepper
1 onion, skinned and finely
    chopped
1 large cauliflower, trimmed and
    broken into tiny florets
1 cooking apple, peeled, cored and
    chopped
100 g (4 oz) frozen peas
10 ml (2 tsp) cornflour
150 ml (¼ pint) natural yogurt
salt and pepper

1. Place the oil, curry powder, mustard, turmeric, cayenne pepper and onion in a large bowl and microwave on HIGH for 5–7 minutes, until the onion has softened, stirring occasionally.

2. Add the cauliflower and apple, cover with cling film, pulling back one corner to allow the steam to escape, and microwave on HIGH for 10–12 minutes until just tender.

3. Stir in the peas.

4. Gradually, blend the yogurt into the cornflour then stir into the cauliflower mixture.

5. Microwave on HIGH for 2 minutes until heated through. Season well with salt and pepper.

MUSHROOMS AND BACON
IN HERB SAUCE

SERVES 4
175 g (6 oz) streaky bacon, rinded
50 g (2 oz) butter or margarine
450 g (1 lb) button mushrooms,
    trimmed and halved
45 ml (3 level tbsp) plain flour
300 ml (½ pint) milk
salt and pepper
15 ml (1 tbsp) lemon juice
30 ml (2 tbsp) chopped fresh
    parsley

1. Lay the bacon in a single layer on a large flat plate. Cover loosely with absorbent kitchen paper and microwave on HIGH for 2–3 minutes until the bacon is cooked. Drain on absorbent kitchen paper, chop roughly and place in a serving dish.

2. Put the butter in a medium bowl and microwave on HIGH for 45 seconds until melted. Stir in the mushrooms and microwave on HIGH for 4–5 minutes until just tender. Remove from the dish with a slotted spoon and mix with the bacon.

3. Stir the flour into the fat remaining in the bowl then gradually stir in the milk. Microwave on HIGH for 4–5 minutes, until thickened, whisking frequently.

4. Season well with salt and pepper and stir in the lemon juice and parsley. Pour over the mushrooms and bacon and mix together carefully.

5. Microwave on HIGH for 1–2 minutes until heated through.

DEVILLED POTATOES

SERVES 4

700 g (1½ lb) potatoes, peeled and
   cut into 2.5 cm (1 inch) squares
50 g (2 oz) butter or margarine
10 ml (2 level tsp) prepared
   mustard
15 ml (1 level tbsp) tomato purée
30 ml (2 tbsp) malt vinegar
15 ml (1 tbsp) Worcestershire
   sauce
salt and pepper

1 Put the potatoes in a large bowl with 30 ml (2 tbsp) water. Cover with cling film, pulling back one corner to allow the steam to escape. Microwave on HIGH for 10 minutes until just tender, stirring occasionally.

2 Drain the potatoes well and return to the bowl. Add the butter to the potatoes and microwave on HIGH for 45 seconds until the butter has melted.

3 Blend the remaining ingredients together, pour over the potatoes and microwave on HIGH for 1 minute until heated through and the potatoes are evenly coated with the sauce.

RED CABBAGE BRAISED WITH ORANGE

SERVES 4–6

25 g (1 oz) butter or margarine
1 medium onion, skinned and
   finely chopped
450 g (1 lb) red cabbage, trimmed
   and very finely shredded
grated rind and juice of 2 oranges
15 ml (1 level tbsp) demerara
   sugar
10 ml (2 tsp) lemon juice
15 ml (1 tbsp) red wine vinegar
75 ml (3 fl oz) chicken stock
salt and pepper

1 Put the butter into a large bowl and microwave on HIGH for 45 seconds until melted. Stir in the onion and microwave on HIGH for 5–7 minutes until softened.

2 Add the cabbage, orange rind and juice, sugar, lemon juice, vinegar, stock, salt and pepper and stir together well.

3 Re-cover and microwave on HIGH for 15–20 minutes until the cabbage is tender.

BUTTERED LEEKS

SERVES 4

450 g (1 lb) leeks, trimmed,
   cut into 1 cm (½ inch) lengths
   and thoroughly washed
300 ml (½ pint) boiling chicken
   stock
75 g (3 oz) butter
salt and pepper
15 ml (1 tbsp) chopped fresh sage
   or parsley

1 Put the leeks in a large bowl with the boiling chicken stock and microwave on HIGH for 12–14 minutes, stirring occasionally, until tender but still crisp. Drain well and return to the bowl.

2 Add the butter and season with salt and pepper. Microwave on HIGH for 2 minutes until the butter has melted. Mix thoroughly and sprinkle with sage or parsley.

POTATO AND PARSLEY BAKE

SERVES 4

25 g (1 oz) butter or margarine
1 medium onion, skinned and
    thinly sliced
1 garlic clove, skinned and crushed
    (optional)
150 ml (¼ pint) soured cream
45 ml (3 tbsp) chopped fresh
    parsley
700 g (1½ lb) potatoes, peeled and
    very thinly sliced
salt and pepper
50 g (2 oz) Cheddar cheese, grated
chopped fresh parsley, to garnish

1 Put the butter in a shallow dish and microwave on HIGH for 30 seconds or until melted.

2 Stir in the onion and garlic, cover with cling film, pulling back one corner to allow the steam to escape, and microwave on HIGH for 5–7 minutes or until the onion has softened.

3 Add the cream, parsley and potatoes, season with salt and pepper then mix together carefully to coat the potato slices with the cream mixture.

4 Re-cover and microwave on HIGH for 15–17 minutes or until the potatoes are tender.

5 Sprinkle the grated cheese over and microwave on HIGH for 1–2 minutes until the cheese has just melted. Brown under a hot grill, if desired.
Serve garnished with chopped parsley.

MINTED CARROTS AND BRUSSELS SPROUTS

SERVES 4

450 g (1 lb) brussels sprouts,
    trimmed
225 g (8 oz) carrots, peeled and
    sliced
50 g (2 oz) butter or
    margarine
30 ml (2 tbsp) chopped fresh
    mint
salt and pepper

1 Put the sprouts and carrots in a large casserole dish or bowl. Add 45 ml (3 tbsp) water and cover with cling film, pulling back one corner to let steam escape. Microwave on HIGH for 9–12 minutes or until tender. Shake the casserole once during the cooking time.

2 Drain the vegetables and return to the casserole.

3 Place the butter or margarine and mint in a small measuring jug and microwave on HIGH for 1 minute or until melted and foaming. Pour the butter over the vegetables and toss until well coated.

4 Microwave on HIGH for 1 minute to reheat if necessary. Season to taste with salt and pepper

DESSERTS

A microwave oven can help with both the preparation (for example, dissolving gelatine and melting chocolate) and the cooking of all manner of desserts from steamed suet puddings to milk puddings and egg custards to cheesecakes.

Light, spongy steamed suet and sponge puddings cook in a fraction of the time needed for conventional steaming. Only half fill the container to allow room for the mixture to rise. Because of the shape of the basin, the top of the pudding will cook before the bottom, so the pudding should be removed from the oven when the surface looks only just cooked. It should then be left to stand so the cooking will even out.

Fruits with skins on, such as apples, should be pierced or slit before cooking and fruit with a high water content, such as rhubarb, will need no additional water but small berries will need a few tablespoonfuls. There is no need to pre-soak dried fruits but sufficient water must be added when cooking to allow fruit to swell to its full size.

BANANA CHEESECAKE

SERVES 6–8

100 g (4 oz) butter or margarine, diced
225 g (8 oz) ginger biscuits, crushed
225 g (8 oz) full fat soft cheese
150 ml ($\frac{1}{4}$ pint) soured cream
3 bananas
30 ml (2 tbsp) clear honey
15 ml (3 level tsp) gelatine
60 ml (4 tbsp) lemon juice
banana slices, to decorate

1 Put the butter in a medium bowl and microwave on HIGH for 1 minute or until melted. Stir in the crushed biscuits and mix together well.

2 Press the mixture over the base of a 20.5 cm (8 inch) loose bottom deep cake tin. Chill for 30 minutes.

3 Meanwhile, beat the cheese and cream together until well mixed. Peel and mash the bananas then beat into the cheese mixture with the honey.

4 Sprinkle the gelatine over the lemon juice in a small bowl and microwave on HIGH for 30–50 seconds, until the gelatine has dissolved, stirring frequently.

5 Stir the dissolved gelatine slowly into the filling then spoon the mixture into the biscuit-lined tin. Chill for 3–4 hours until the filling is set.

6 Remove the cheesecake carefully from the tin and place on a serving plate. Immediately before serving, peel and slice the banana for the decoration and arrange the slices around the edge of the cheesecake.

CREAMY RICE PUDDING

SERVES 3–4
butter for greasing
225 ml (8 fl oz) full cream
evaporated milk
50 g (2 oz) short grain rice
25 g (1 oz) caster sugar

1 Butter a large bowl. Mix the milk and 350 ml (12 fl oz) water together. Pour into the bowl and stir in the rice and sugar. Cover with cling film, pulling back one corner to allow the steam to escape.

2 Microwave on HIGH for 5–6 minutes or until the liquid is boiling.

3 Immediately reduce to LOW and cook for 35–40 minutes, or until starting to thicken. Stir with a fork to break up any lumps of rice after every 15 minutes and at the end of the cooking time.

4 Leave to stand for 5 minutes to thicken further before serving.

VARIATIONS:
Add 50 g (2 oz) sultanas or raisins to the ingredients and proceed as above.

After cooking in the microwave oven, turn the rice into a shallow heatproof dish and sprinkle with demerara sugar. Place under a preheated conventional grill until the sugar has caramelised.

BREAD PUDDING

SERVES 6
225 g (8 oz) stale bread, broken
into small pieces
450 ml (¾ pint) milk
175 g (6 oz) mixed dried fruit
50 g (2 oz) shredded suet
10 ml (2 level tsp) ground mixed
spice
65 g (2½ oz) soft dark brown sugar
1 egg, beaten
freshly grated nutmeg
caster or brown sugar, to dredge
custard (see page 82), to serve

1 Grease a 900 ml (1½ pint) shallow round dish.

2 Put the bread into the dish, pour the milk over and leave to soak for 30 minutes. Beat out the lumps.

3 Add the dried fruit, suet, spice and the sugar and mix together well. Stir in the egg, and mix to a soft dropping consistency, adding a little more milk if necessary.

4 Spread the mixture evenly in the dish and grate a little nutmeg over the surface.

5 Microwave on MEDIUM for 10–15 minutes until the mixture is almost set in the middle, giving the dish a quarter turn four times during cooking if the oven does not have a turntable.

6 Leave to stand for 10 minutes. Dredge with caster or brown sugar.
Serve warm or cold with custard.

FRUITY SUET PUDDING

SERVES 4–6

175 g (6 oz) cooking apples, peeled,
    quartered and sliced
175 g (6 oz) plums, halved and
    stones removed
225 g (8 oz) blackberries, hulls
    removed
finely grated rind of 1 lemon
15 ml (1 tbsp) lemon juice
100 g (4 oz) plus 15 ml
    (1 level tbsp) caster sugar
175 g (6 oz) self raising flour
75 g (3 oz) shredded suet
milk, to mix
custard (see page 82) or ice cream,
    to serve

1 | Grease a 1.4 litre (2½ pint) microwave pudding basin. Line the bottom of the basin with a circle of greaseproof paper.

2 | Put the prepared fruits in three separate bowls. Add the lemon rind and juice and 50 g (2 oz) of the sugar to the apples and add the remaining 50 g (2 oz) sugar, to taste, equally between the plums and the blackberries. Mix the fruits and the sugar together.

3 | To make the suetcrust pastry, put the flour and the 15 ml (1 level tbsp) sugar into a mixing bowl and mix in the shredded suet. Bind the ingredients together with 60–75 ml (4–5 tbsp) milk to form a soft but not sticky dough.

4 | Turn the dough out on to a lightly floured surface and shape into a flat cylinder, wider at one end than the other. Cut into four pieces.

5 | Shape the smallest piece of pastry into a round large enough to fit the bottom of the prepared pudding basin. Place it in the bottom of the basin and spoon in the apple mixture.

6 | Shape a slightly larger piece of pastry into a round large enough to cover the apples. Place on top of the apples and spoon the plums on top. Repeat with another round to cover the plums and spoon in the blackberries.

7 | Shape the remaining pastry into a round large enough to cover the blackberries. Cover the blackberries with this final layer of pastry. There should be space above the last layer of pastry to allow it to rise during cooking.

8 | Cover the pudding basin with cling film, pleated in the centre to allow for expansion. Microwave on HIGH for 15–16 minutes. Allow the pudding to stand in the basin, covered, for 5 minutes before turning it out carefully on to a hot serving dish.
    Serve hot with custard or ice cream.

SPONGE PUDDING

SERVES 3–4

50 g (2 oz) soft tub margarine
50 g (2 oz) caster sugar
1 egg, beaten
few drops of vanilla flavouring
100 g (4 oz) self raising flour
45–60 ml (3–4 tbsp) milk
custard (see page 82), to serve

1 Beat the margarine, sugar, egg, vanilla flavouring and flour until smooth. Gradually stir in enough milk to give a soft dropping consistency.

2 Spoon into a greased 600 ml (1 pint) pudding basin and level the surface. Cover with a plate.

3 Microwave on HIGH for 5–7 minutes until the top of the sponge is only slightly moist and a wooden cocktail stick inserted in the centre comes out clean.

4 Leave to stand for 5 minutes before turning out on to a heated serving dish.
Serve with custard.

VARIATIONS
Essex pudding
Spread jam over the sides and base of the greased pudding basin.
Apricot sponge pudding
Drain a 411 g (14½ oz) can of apricot halves and arrange them in the base of the greased pudding basin.
Syrup sponge pudding
Put 30 ml (2 tbsp) golden syrup into the bottom of the basin before adding the mixture. Flavour the mixture with the grated rind of a lemon.
Chocolate sponge pudding
Blend 60 ml (4 level tbsp) cocoa powder to a smooth cream with 15 ml (1 tbsp) hot water and add to the beaten ingredients.
Jamaica pudding
Add 50–100 g (2–4 oz) chopped stem ginger with the milk.
Lemon or orange sponge
Add the grated rind of 1 orange or lemon when beating the ingredients.

HOT SHERRIED GRAPEFRUIT

SERVES 4

2 grapefruit, cut in half
60 ml (4 tbsp) sherry or kirsch
30 ml (2 level tbsp) brown sugar
2 maraschino cherries, cut in half,
to decorate

1 Loosen the segments of each grapefruit half with a serrated knife or grapefruit knife. Put in individual serving dishes.

2 Pour 15 ml (1 tbsp) sherry or kirsch over each grapefruit half and sprinkle with brown sugar.

3 Arrange the serving dishes in a circle in the oven and microwave on HIGH for about 2 minutes until hot. Decorate with the halved cherries.

STUFFED BAKED APPLES

SERVES 4
4 medium cooking apples, cored
60 ml (4 tbsp) mincemeat

1 With the point of a sharp knife, make a slit in the skin around the middle of each apple. Put in individual dishes or a round serving dish.

2 Fill the centre of each apple with mincemeat.

3 Cover the apples loosely with greaseproof paper and place in the oven, arranging individual dishes in a circle.

4 Microwave on HIGH for 5½–7½ minutes until the fruit is just cooked, but still holds its shape.

5 Leave to stand, covered, for 5 minutes before serving.

NOTE:
Cook one apple on HIGH for 2½–3 minutes. Cook two apples on HIGH for 3½–4½ minutes.

SEMOLINA PUDDING

SERVES 2–3
568 ml (1 pint) milk
60 ml (4 level tbsp) semolina or
  ground rice
30 ml (2 level tbsp) caster sugar

1 Put the milk, semolina and sugar in a large bowl. Microwave on HIGH for 5–6 minutes or until the milk boils. Stir thoroughly.

2 Three-quarters cover with cling film or a lid and microwave on HIGH for 1–2 minutes until returned to the boil. Reduce to LOW and microwave for 10–15 minutes until thickened, stirring frequently.

3 Leave to stand, covered, for 5 minutes. Stir before serving.

SPOTTED DICK

SERVES 4
75 g (3 oz) self-raising flour
pinch of salt
75 g (3 oz) fresh breadcrumbs
75 g (3 oz) shredded suet
50 g (2 oz) soft light brown sugar
175 g (6 oz) currants
about 90 ml (6 tbsp) milk
custard (see page 82), to serve

1 Mix the flour, salt, breadcrumbs, suet, sugar and currants in a large bowl. Stir in enough milk to give a soft dropping consistency.

2 Spoon into a 900 ml (1½ pint) pudding basin and cover loosely with cling film. Microwave on HIGH for 5 minutes. Leave to stand, covered for 5 minutes, then turn out on to a hot serving plate.
    Serve with custard.

SAUCY CHOCOLATE PUDDING

SERVES 4

100 g (4 oz) plain flour
75 ml (5 level tbsp) cocoa powder
10 ml (2 level tsp) baking powder
pinch of salt
275 g (10 oz) soft light brown
    sugar
175 ml (6 fl oz) milk
30 ml (2 tbsp) vegetable oil
5 ml (1 tsp) vanilla flavouring
50 g (2 oz) walnuts, finely chopped
    (optional)

1   Sift the flour, 10 ml (2 level tsp) cocoa, the baking powder and the salt into a large bowl. Stir in 100 g (4 oz) of the sugar.

2   Make a well in the centre and pour in the milk, oil and vanilla flavouring. Beat to a smooth batter. Stir in the nuts, if using.

3   Pour the mixture into a 20.5 cm (8 inch) round dish.

4   Mix the remaining sugar and cocoa together, sprinkle evenly over the batter and pour 350 ml (12 fl oz) boiling water over.

5   Microwave on HIGH for 12–14 minutes or until the top looks dry and the sauce is just bubbling through – the pudding will have separated into a light sponge on top leaving a rich chocolate sauce underneath. Give the dish a quarter turn four times during cooking if the oven does not have a turntable.

6   Serve immediately.

APPLE CRUMBLE

SERVES 4

100 g (4 oz) butter or margarine,
    chopped
175 g (6 oz) flour
100 g (4 oz) granulated or
    demerara sugar
700 g (1½ lb) cooking apples,
    peeled, cored and thinly sliced
pinch of ground cloves

1   Rub the butter into the flour until the mixture resembles fine breadcrumbs. Stir in 50 g (2 oz) of the sugar.

2   Spread the apples evenly in a shallow dish. Sprinkle with the remaining sugar and ground cloves.

3   Cover and microwave on HIGH for 5 minutes until the apples begin to soften.

4   Sprinkle the crumble mixture over the fruit to completely cover it.

5   Without covering, microwave on HIGH for 10–12 minutes until just set giving the dish a quarter turn during cooking if the oven does not have a turntable.

6   Brown under a hot grill, if desired.

STRAWBERRY FOOL

SERVES 6
30–45 ml (2–3 level tbsp) sugar
20 ml (4 level tsp) cornflour
300 ml (½ pint) milk
700 g (1½ lb) strawberries, hulled
300 ml (½ pint) double cream

1 Blend 15 ml (1 level tbsp) of the sugar and the cornflour with a little of the milk in a measuring jug or medium bowl. Stir in the remainder of the milk.

2 Microwave on HIGH for 3–4 minutes until thickened, stirring every minute. Cover the surface of the sauce closely with cling film and leave until cold.

3 Reserve a few whole strawberries for decoration. Push the remaining strawberries through a nylon sieve to form a purée or put in a blender or food processor and purée until smooth, then push through a nylon sieve to remove the pips.

4 Stir the cold sauce into the strawberry purée. Mix well and sweeten to taste with the remaining sugar.

5 Lightly whip the cream and fold into the strawberry mixture. Turn into six individual dishes and chill for 1–2 hours.

6 Thinly slice the reserved strawberries and arrange on top of each portion, to decorate.

ORANGE WATER ICE

SERVES 4
100 g (4 oz) caster sugar
juice of 3 oranges
finely grated rind and juice of
  1 lemon
1 egg white

1 Put the sugar and 300 ml (½ pint) water in a large bowl and microwave on HIGH for 3–4 minutes, stirring occasionally, until the sugar has dissolved and the syrup is boiling.

2 Microwave on HIGH for a further 8 minutes. Strain the orange juice and the lemon juice into the syrup then stir in the lemon rind. Leave until cold.

3 Pour into a shallow metal container, cover and freeze for 1–1½ hours until slushy.

4 Whisk the egg white until stiff. Turn the slushy mixture into a cold bowl then fold in the egg white. Return the mixture to the container, cover and freeze for 3–4 hours until firm.

5 Transfer to the refrigerator 30–40 minutes before serving to soften slightly.

BAKING

Microwave ovens produce light, even-textured cakes but because the sugar in them does not caramelise and form a crust on the surface, and because the mixtures are always moist, the cakes do not brown but they rise higher than cakes baked in a conventional oven and have a more open, airy texture. However, if the mixture contains ingredients that colour it the lack of extra browning will not matter. The cake mixture should be very moist and cooked in a round, straight-sided container, such as an ovenproof glass soufflé dish, or a ring mould for large cakes. Line the bottom of the container with greaseproof paper and only fill the container about half full. Cook small cakes in small paper cases — use 2 per cake for extra support and stand in a muffin pan, ramekins or cups to support the paper cases. Arrange in a circle in the oven.

Remove the cake from the oven when it is still moist on the top and in the centre (normally it would be considered slightly underdone) then let it stand for 5—15 minutes, depending on the size and texture, to complete cooking. Good results can be obtained with moist cookie-type biscuits such as flap-jacks and brownies but it is not possible to make traditional crisp biscuits.

When cooking a number of small cakes or biscuits arrange them in a circle about 5 cm (2 inches) apart.

BRAN TEA BREAD

MAKES ONE 20 × 12.5 cm
(8 × 5 inch) LOAF
100 g (4 oz) bran breakfast cereal
(not flaked)
75 g (3 oz) soft dark brown sugar
225 g (8 oz) mixed dried fruit
50 g (2 oz) nuts, chopped
300 ml (½ pint) milk
100 g (4 oz) self raising flour
5 ml (1 level tsp) mixed spice

1 Grease a 20 × 12.5 × 6 cm (8 × 5 × 2½ inch) loaf dish and line the base with greaseproof paper.

2 Put the bran cereal, sugar, fruit and nuts in a bowl. Pour the milk over and leave to soak for 1½—2 hours, until the liquid has been absorbed.

3 Stir in the flour and spice, mixing together well.

4 Turn the mixture into the prepared dish. Press down firmly and level the surface.

5 Microwave on LOW for 14—16 minutes until a wooden cocktail stick inserted into the centre comes out clean. Give the dish a quarter turn four times during cooking if the oven is not fitted with a turntable.

6 Leave to stand for 5 minutes before turning out to cool on a wire rack.

7 When cold, wrap and store for 1—2 days. Serve sliced and buttered.

IRISH SODA BREAD

MAKES ONE 450 g (1 lb) LOAF
450 g (1 lb) wholemeal flour,
    plus a little extra for sifting
5 ml (1 level tsp) salt
5 ml (1 level tsp) bicarbonate of
    soda
15 g (½ oz) butter or margarine
10 ml (2 level tsp) cream of tartar
5 ml (1 level tsp) dark brown sugar
300 ml (½ pint) milk, plus a little
    extra for glazing
cheese and pickles, to serve

1 Lightly grease a large, flat plate or microwave baking tray.

2 Mix the flour, salt and bicarbonate of soda in a mixing bowl and rub in the butter until the mixture resembles fine breadcrumbs.

3 Dissolve the cream of tartar and sugar in the milk and use to bind the flour together to form a firm dough, adding a little more milk if necessary.

4 Knead the dough on a lightly floured surface until firm and smooth and there are no cracks.

5 Flatten out the dough to a round about 18 cm (7 inches) in diameter and place on the prepared plate or tray.

6 Brush the surface of the dough with a little milk and mark a deep cross in the top with a knife. Sift a little flour on top.

7 Microwave on HIGH for 9 minutes, giving the dish a quarter turn three times during cooking, until well risen and dry on the top, then turn over and microwave on HIGH for 1–1½ minutes or until the surface is firm.

8 Cool on a wire rack for 5 minutes.
Serve immediately with cheese and pickles.

CHOCOLATE BISCUIT CAKE

SERVES 8
100 g (4 oz) plain chocolate,
    broken into small pieces
100 g (4 oz) butter, diced
15 ml (1 level tbsp) golden syrup
30 ml (2 tbsp) double cream
125 g (4 oz) digestive biscuits,
    finely broken up
50 g (2 oz) raisins
50 g (2 oz) glacé cherries, quartered
50 g (2 oz) flaked almonds, toasted

1 Butter a 20.5 cm (8 inch) shallow glass dish.

2 Put the chocolate, butter, syrup and cream into a large bowl. Microwave on LOW for 5 minutes until the chocolate and butter have melted.

3 Cool slightly, then mix in the biscuits, fruit and nuts.

4 Turn the mixture into the prepared dish, lightly level the top, then chill for at least 1 hour.

5 Serve cut into wedges.

LEMON AND HAZELNUT CAKE

MAKES ONE 18 cm (7 inch) CAKE
100 g (4 oz) butter or margarine
150 g (5 oz) caster sugar
finely grated rind and juice of
  1 lemon
2 eggs, beaten
75 g (3 oz) self raising flour
50 g (2 oz) ground hazelnuts
30 ml (2 tbsp) milk

For the filling:
300 ml (½ pint) double cream

1 Base-line an 18 cm (7 inch) soufflé dish.

2 Cream the butter and 100 g (4 oz) sugar until light and fluffy. Add the grated lemon rind and gradually beat in the eggs.

3 Fold in the flour, half the hazelnuts and the milk.

4 Turn the mixture into the prepared dish. Smooth the top. Microwave on HIGH for 4–5 minutes until a wooden cocktail stick inserted in the centre comes out clean.

5 Leave to stand for 10 minutes then turn out on to a cooling rack.

6 Mix the lemon juice with the remaining caster sugar. Pour over the top of the cake while still warm and sprinkle with the remaining hazelnuts. Leave to cool completely.

7 Lightly whip the cream. Cut the cake in half then sandwich the two halves together with the cream.

DATE AND WALNUT FLAPJACKS

MAKES 8
225 g (8 oz) dates, stoned and
  finely chopped
30 ml (2 level tbsp) clear honey
100 g (4 oz) butter or margarine,
  chopped
75 g (3 oz) wholemeal flour
100 g (4 oz) soft dark brown sugar
pinch of salt
75 g (3 oz) rolled oats
50 g (2 oz) walnuts, finely chopped

1 Put the dates in a medium bowl, add the honey and 75 ml (3 fl oz) water and microwave on HIGH for 5 minutes. Cover and leave to stand.

2 Rub the butter into the flour until the mixture resembles fine breadcrumbs. Stir in the sugar, salt, oats and walnuts.

3 Press half the mixture into the base of a 20.5 cm (8 inch) shallow glass dish. Microwave on MEDIUM for 4 minutes.

4 Spoon the dates evenly over the cooked mixture and sprinkle with the remaining oat mixture. Microwave on HIGH for 6 minutes.

5 Mark into 8 wedges while warm and leave to cool in the dish. When cold turn out and cut into wedges.

WHOLEMEAL LOAF

MAKES ONE 450 g (1 lb) LOAF
5 ml (1 level tsp) caster sugar
5 ml (1 level tsp) dried yeast
450 g (1 lb) wholemeal flour
2.5 ml (½ level tsp) salt
15 g (½ oz) butter or margarine,
   chopped
15 ml (1 level tbsp) bran

1 Grease a 450 g (1 lb) loaf dish.

2 Mix the sugar and dried yeast with 100 ml (4 fl oz) hand-hot water and leave in a warm place for about 10 minutes until frothy.

3 Put the flour and salt in a mixing bowl and microwave on HIGH for about 30 seconds until warm.

4 Rub the butter into the flour then mix to a soft dough with the yeast liquid and about 175 ml (6 fl oz) water.

5 Turn the dough on to a lightly floured surface and knead until smooth. Shape into a loaf and place in the prepared container.

6 Cover with a lightly oiled polythene bag and leave in a warm place until doubled in size.

7 Remove the bag, sprinkle the top of the loaf with the bran, and microwave on HIGH for 6 minutes until a wooden cocktail stick inserted in the centre comes out clean.

8 Turn out of the container and brown under a hot grill for a few minutes, if desired.

PEANUT FUDGE SQUARES

MAKES ABOUT 25 SQUARES
115 g (4½ oz) unsalted butter
225 g (8 oz) icing sugar
225 g (8 oz) peanut butter
100 g (4 oz) unsalted peanuts
50 g (2 oz) raisins, roughly
   chopped
175 g (6 oz) plain chocolate,
   broken into small pieces

1 Cut 100 g (4 oz) of the butter into small pieces and put in a large bowl. Microwave on HIGH for 1 minute until melted.

2 Add the icing sugar, peanut butter, peanuts and raisins to the melted butter and mix well.

3 Transfer the mixture to an 18 × 28 × 2.5 cm (7 × 11 × 1 inch) deep tin and pat down with the back of a wooden spoon.

4 Put the chocolate into a bowl with the remaining 15 g (½ oz) of butter. Microwave on HIGH for 2 minutes until melted. Mix together and spread evenly over the top of the peanut butter mixture.

5 Mark into squares and chill for 10–15 minutes. Remove from the tin and cut into squares.

VICTORIA SANDWICH CAKE

SERVES 6–8
175 g (6 oz) self raising flour
175 g (6 oz) butter or margarine,
  softened
175 g (6 oz) caster sugar
3 eggs
30–45 ml (2–3 tbsp) milk
jam, to fill
icing sugar, for dusting

1 Grease a 19 cm (7½ inch) deep soufflé dish and line the base with greased greaseproof paper.

2 Mix the flour, butter, sugar, eggs and 30 ml (2 tbsp) milk together in a medium bowl. Beat until smooth. If necessary, add an extra 15 ml (1 tbsp) milk to give a soft dropping consistency.

3 Spoon the mixture into the prepared dish and microwave on HIGH for 5½–7½ minutes until a wooden cocktail stick inserted into the centre comes out clean.

4 Leave to stand for 10 minutes then turn out on to a wire rack, remove the lining paper and leave to cool.

5 When the cake is completely cold, split it in half and sandwich together with jam. Sift icing sugar over the top of the cake.

VARIATIONS
Orange or lemon
Replace the milk with the juice and the grated rind of 1 orange or 1 lemon and proceed as above. When cold, split and fill with orange or lemon flavoured butter cream.

Chocolate
Replace 45 ml (3 level tbsp) of flour by 45 ml (3 level tbsp) of cocoa powder. Sandwich together with vanilla or chocolate butter cream. For a more moist cake, blend the cocoa powder with water to give a thick paste. Mix into the beaten ingredients.

Coffee
Dissolve 10 ml (2 level tsp) instant coffee in a little warm water and the milk, then add to the remaining ingredients. Or use 10 ml (2 tsp) coffee essence.

Vanilla Butter Cream
Sift 225 g (8 oz) icing sugar into a bowl then gradually beat in 100 g (4 oz) softened butter, adding a few drops of vanilla essence and 15–30 ml (1–2 tbsp) milk. **For chocolate butter cream** beat in 15 ml (1 level tbsp) cocoa powder dissolved in a little hot water then left to cool. Omit the milk.
For coffee butter cream, omit the vanilla essence but add 10 ml (2 tsp) instant coffee powder dissolved in a little of the milk.

QUICK ROLLS

MAKES 10 ROLLS
225 g (8 oz) plain wholemeal flour
10 ml (2 level tsp) baking powder
2.5 ml (½ level tsp) salt
25 g (1 oz) butter or margarine
about 150 ml (¼ pint) milk
45 ml (3 tbsp) coarse oatmeal or
*   cracked wheat*

1 Put the flour, baking powder and salt into a large bowl. Rub in the butter until the mixture resembles fine breadcrumbs.

2 Make a well in the centre, add the milk and mix with a round-bladed knife to give a fairly soft dough. Add a little extra milk if necessary.

3 Draw the mixture together and turn on to a lightly floured board. Divide into ten portions and shape into rolls.

4 Flatten the top of each roll then brush with water and sprinkle with the coarse oatmeal or cracked wheat.

5 Place the rolls on two large, flat plates, five to a plate. Microwave one plate at a time on HIGH for 3 minutes or until risen.

6 Cool on a wire cooling rack. These are best eaten while still warm.

BOSTON BROWNIES

MAKES 24 SQUARES
100 g (4 oz) plain chocolate,
*   chopped*
100 g (4 oz) butter or margarine,
*   diced*
100 g (4 oz) soft dark brown sugar
100 g (4 oz) self raising flour
10 ml (2 level tsp) cocoa powder
1.25 ml (¼ level tsp) salt
2 eggs, size 2, beaten
2.5 ml (½ tsp) vanilla flavouring
100 g (4 oz) walnuts, roughly
*   chopped*

1 Grease two shallow 12.5 cm (5 inch) × 18 cm (7 inch) glass ovenproof dishes or plastic dishes. Line the base with greaseproof paper.

2 Put the chocolate and butter into a large heat-proof bowl. Microwave on LOW for 3–5 minutes until the chocolate is soft and glossy on top and the butter has melted. Stir well until smooth.

3 Stir the sugar into the chocolate mixture. Sift the flour, cocoa and salt into the bowl. Add the eggs and vanilla flavouring and beat well to make a smooth batter. Stir in the walnuts.

4 Pour half of the brownie mixture into one of the prepared dishes and cover each end of the dish with a small piece of foil, shiny side down. Cover with cling film and microwave on HIGH for 5 minutes until well risen, firm to the touch and slightly moist on the surface. If the cooker has no turntable give the dish a quarter turn three times during cooking. Repeat with the remaining mixture.

5 Remove the cling film and foil and allow the mixture to cool in the dish. Cut each cake into about twelve squares before serving.

CHOCOLATE LOAF CAKE

MAKES ONE 23cm (9 inch)
LOAF-SHAPED CAKE
100 g (4 oz) golden syrup
100 g (4 oz) soft dark brown sugar
100 g (4 oz) butter or margarine
175 g (6 oz) self raising flour
50 g (2 oz) cocoa powder
1 egg, beaten
150 ml (¼ pint) milk
100 g (4 oz) plain chocolate,
  broken into small pieces
25 g (1 oz) flaked almonds

1 Grease a 23 cm (9 inch) loaf dish and line with greaseproof paper.

2 Put the syrup, brown sugar and butter in a large bowl and microwave on HIGH for 2 minutes or until the butter has melted and the sugar dissolved, stirring occasionally.

3 Sift in the flour and cocoa and mix together well.

4 Beat in the eggs then stir in the milk.

5 Turn the mixture into the prepared dish and microwave on HIGH for 5 minutes until a wooden cocktail stick inserted into the centre comes out clean.

6 Leave to stand for 5 minutes before turning out to cool completely.

7 Put the chocolate into a small bowl and microwave on HIGH for about 1 minute until melted, stirring occasionally.

8 Spread the melted chocolate over the top of the cake, allowing it to trickle over the edges and sides. Leave to set, then sprinkle the flaked almonds over the top.

ENGLISH MADELEINES

MAKES 8
100 g (4 oz) butter or margarine
100 g (4 oz) caster sugar
2 eggs, size 2, beaten
100 g (4 oz) self raising flour
75 ml (5 level tbsp) red jam, sieved
40 g (1½ oz) desiccated coconut
4 glacé cherries, halved,
  and angelica pieces, to decorate

1 Grease 8 paper drinking cups. Line the base of each one with a round of greaseproof paper.

2 Cream the butter and the sugar together until very pale and fluffy. Add the eggs a little at a time, beating well after each addition. Carefully fold in the flour.

3 Divide the mixture evenly among the prepared cups. Place the cups on flat heatproof plates, 4 to each plate.

4 Cover with cling film and microwave one plate at a time for 1½–2 minutes until the mixture is cooked but just slightly moist on the surface. Quickly remove the cling film. Stand for 1–2 minutes, then carefully turn the cakes out on to a rack to cool.

5 When the cakes are almost cold, trim the bases, if necessary, so that they stand firmly and are about the same height.

6 Put the jam in a small heatproof bowl and microwave on HIGH for 1–2 minutes until melted and boiling; stir well.

7 Spread the coconut out on a large plate. Spear each cake on to a skewer, brush them with the boiling jam and then roll them in the coconut until they are evenly coated.

8 Top each madeleine with half a glacé cherry and small pieces of angelica.

RICH FRUIT CAKE

MAKES ONE 20.5 cm (8 inch) CAKE
2 eggs
100 g (4 oz) soft dark brown sugar
30 ml (2 tbsp) black treacle
60 ml (4 tbsp) vegetable oil
175 g (6 oz) self raising flour
2.5 ml ($\frac{1}{2}$ level tsp) baking powder
5 ml (1 level tsp) mixed spice
pinch of salt
100 ml (4 fl oz) milk
700 g (1$\frac{1}{2}$ lb) mixed dried fruit
50 g (2 oz) glacé cherries, quartered
100 g (4 oz) mixed chopped nuts
30 ml (2 tbsp) brandy
30 ml (2 level tbsp) apricot jam,
    to decorate
8 walnut halves, to decorate
8 glacé cherries, halved, to decorate

1 Base-line a 20.5 cm (8 inch) round soufflé dish.

2 Beat the eggs, sugar, treacle and oil together in a large mixing bowl.

3 Sieve the dry ingredients together then stir into the mixture with the milk. Stir in the fruit and nuts.

4 Spoon the mixture into the prepared dish and level the top.

5 Microwave on LOW for 30–40 minutes until a wooden cocktail stick inserted in the centre comes out clean. Give the dish a quarter turn four times during cooking if the oven does not have a turntable.

6 Leave in the dish to cool for 30 minutes then turn out on to a cooling rack and leave to cool completely.

7 When cold, prick the cake with a fine skewer and pour the brandy over. Wrap in greaseproof paper and then aluminium foil. Leave to mature for about one week.

8 To decorate, put the jam in a small bowl and microwave on HIGH for 1 minute until melted. Spread the jam over the cake and arrange the walnut and cherry halves on top.

SAUCES

Making sauces in a microwave cooker is worthwhile for the simplicity, convenience and saving on washing up, even though there is little saving in time.

Providing an occasional stir is given to the sauce, there is very little risk of lumps forming or of burning occurring. As the ingredients can be mixed together in the cooking and serving dish, there is minimal washing up. Furthermore, if the sauce is made in advance, it can be left to cool in the same container (cover the surface of the sauce closely with greaseproof paper to prevent a skin forming) and reheated when required. Remove the greaseproof paper before reheating and stir the sauce occasionally.

When making sauces thickened with cornflour or arrowroot, make sure the thickening agent is completely dissolved in cold liquid before adding a hot one. Sauces thickened with egg are best cooked on a LOW or MEDIUM setting (if your cooker has a variable power control) as care is needed to prevent them curdling.

BARBECUE SAUCE

SERVES 4
50 g (2 oz) butter or margarine
1 large onion, skinned and chopped
5 ml (1 level tsp) tomato purée
30 ml (2 tbsp) malt vinegar
30 ml (2 level tbsp) demerara sugar
10 ml (2 level tsp) mustard powder
30 ml (2 tbsp) Worcestershire sauce

1 Put the butter into a medium heatproof bowl. Microwave on HIGH for 1 minute until melted.

2 Stir in the onion and microwave on HIGH for 5–7 minutes until softened.

3 Whisk all the remaining ingredients together with 150 ml ($\frac{1}{4}$ pint) water then stir them into the onion. Microwave uncovered on HIGH for 5 minutes, stirring frequently. Serve hot.

BREAD SAUCE

SERVES 6
6 cloves
1 medium onion, skinned
4 black peppercorns
few blades of mace
450 ml ($\frac{3}{4}$ pint) milk
25 g (1 oz) butter or margarine
100 g (4 oz) fresh breadcrumbs
salt and pepper
30 ml (2 tbsp) single cream (optional)

1 Stick the cloves into the onion and place in a medium heatproof bowl with the peppercorns and mace. Pour in the milk. Microwave on HIGH for 5 minutes, stirring occasionally, until hot.

2 Remove from the oven, cover and leave to infuse for at least 30 minutes.

3 Discard the peppercorns and mace and add the butter or margarine and breadcrumbs to the bowl. Mix well and cover with cling film, pulling back one corner to allow the steam to escape. Microwave on HIGH for 3 minutes until thickened, whisking after every minute. Remove the onion, season to taste with salt and pepper and stir in the cream, if using. Leave to stand for 2 minutes.

Serve with roast chicken, turkey or game dishes.

WHITE SAUCE

MAKES 300 ml (½ pint)
Pouring sauce:
15 g (½ oz) butter or margarine
15 g (½ oz) plain flour
300 ml (½ pint) milk
salt and pepper
Coating sauce:
25 g (1 oz) butter or margarine
25 g (1 oz) plain flour
300 ml (½ pint) milk
salt and pepper

1 Put all the ingredients in a measuring jug or medium bowl and blend well together.

2 Microwave on HIGH for 4–5 minutes or until the sauce has boiled and thickened, whisking after every minute. Season with salt and pepper.

Variations

Add the following to the hot sauce with the seasoning:

Cheese sauce: 50 g (2 oz) grated mature Cheddar cheese and a pinch of mustard powder.

Parsley sauce: 30 ml (2 tbsp) chopped fresh parsley.

Hot tartare sauce: 15 ml (1 tbsp) chopped fresh parsley, 10 ml (2 tsp) chopped gherkins, 10 ml (2 tsp) chopped capers and 15 ml (1 tbsp) lemon juice.

Caper sauce: 15 ml (1 tbsp) capers and 5–10 ml (1–2 tsp) vinegar from the jar of capers.

Blue cheese sauce: 50 g (2 oz) crumbled Stilton or other blue cheese and 10 ml (2 tsp) lemon juice.

Mushroom sauce: 75 g (3 oz) sliced, lightly cooked mushrooms.

Onion sauce: 1 medium chopped, cooked onion.

Egg sauce: 1 finely chopped hard-boiled egg.

CURRY SAUCE

SERVES 6
50 g (2 oz) butter or margarine, diced
1 medium onion, skinned and finely chopped
15–20 ml (3–4 level tsp) mild curry powder
45 ml (3 level tbsp) plain flour
450 ml (¾ pint) milk or half stock and half milk
30 ml (2 level tbsp) mango or apple chutney, roughly chopped
salt and pepper

1 Put the butter in a medium heatproof bowl, and microwave on HIGH for 1 minute until melted.

2 Stir in the onion and microwave on HIGH for 5–7 minutes until softened.

3 Stir in the flour and curry powder and microwave on HIGH for 30 seconds. Gradually stir in the milk or milk and stock.

4 Cover the bowl with cling film, pulling back one corner to allow the steam to escape. Microwave on HIGH for 5 minutes, stirring every minute, until the sauce is boiling and thickened.

5 Add the chutney and season with salt and pepper. Microwave on HIGH for 30 seconds to reheat.

Serve with vegetables such as marrow or cabbage wedges, or hard-boiled eggs or mix with cooked fish, chicken or meat.

MEAT SAUCE

SERVES 4

15 ml (1 tbsp) vegetable oil
1 large onion, skinned and finely
  chopped
1 garlic clove, skinned and crushed
100 g (4 oz) streaky bacon, rinded
  and chopped
450 g (1 lb) lean minced beef
397 g (14 oz) can tomatoes
100 g (4 oz) mushrooms, sliced
5 ml (1 tsp) Worcestershire sauce
30 ml (2 level tbsp) tomato purée
5 ml (1 level tsp) dried mixed herbs
pinch of nutmeg
salt and pepper

1 Heat the oil in a large bowl on HIGH for 30–60 seconds.

2 Stir in the onion, garlic and bacon, cover with cling film and microwave on HIGH for 5–7 minutes until the onion has softened.

3 Break up the meat and stir in. Cover and cook on HIGH for 2–3 minutes or until the meat is no longer pink. Drain off any excess fat.

4 Add the tomatoes and their juice, roughly break them up, then add the remaining ingredients.

5 Cover with cling film, pulling back one corner to allow the steam to escape. Microwave on HIGH for a further 15–20 minutes or until cooked, stirring after 10 minutes if there is no turntable.

SERVING SUGGESTIONS

1 Over cooked rice or pasta, sprinkled with Parmesan cheese.

2 As a base for Shepherd's Pie – top with hot cooked mashed potato and brown under a hot grill.

3 As a sauce for pasta or rice – add 150 ml ($\frac{1}{4}$ pint) red wine or stock at the end of step 3, bring to the boil and cook uncovered until thickened and reduced, stirring occasionally.

TUNA AND ONION SAUCE

SERVES 4

25 g (1 oz) butter or margarine
1 large onion, skinned and finely
  chopped
198 g (7 oz) can tuna fish, drained
  and flaked
60 ml (4 tbsp) chicken stock
45 ml (3 tbsp) soured cream
2.5 ml ($\frac{1}{2}$ level tsp) paprika
salt and pepper

1 Put the butter or margarine in a medium heat-proof bowl and microwave on HIGH for 45 seconds until melted. Stir in the onion and microwave on HIGH for 5–7 minutes until softened.

2 Add the tuna fish, stock and soured cream and stir gently. Microwave on HIGH for 3 minutes until hot. Add the paprika and season to taste with salt and pepper.

Serve with pasta and Parmesan cheese or freshly cooked vegetables, such as French beans.

TOMATO SAUCE

MAKES 450 ml (¾ pint)
25 g (1 oz) butter or margarine
1 large onion, skinned and finely
  chopped
1 celery stick, trimmed and finely
  chopped
1 carrot, peeled and finely chopped
1 garlic clove, skinned and crushed
397 g (14 oz) can tomatoes
150 ml (¼ pint) chicken stock
15 ml (1 level tbsp) tomato purée
5 ml (1 level tsp) granulated sugar
2.5 ml (½ level tsp) dried mixed
  herbs
salt and pepper

1 Put the butter in a large bowl and microwave on HIGH for 45 seconds until melted. Add the onion, celery, carrot and garlic and microwave on HIGH for 5–7 minutes until the vegetables have softened.

2 Stir in the tomatoes and their juice, the stock, tomato purée, sugar and herbs. Season with salt and pepper. Microwave on HIGH for 10 minutes or until the sauce has thickened, stirring once or twice during the cooking time.

3 Leave to cool slightly, then purée in a blender or food processor. Pour the sauce back into the bowl and reheat on HIGH for 2 minutes.

Serve hot with pasta, chops, or over vegetables.

EGG CUSTARD SAUCE

MAKES 300 ml (½ pint)
300 ml (½ pint) milk
2 eggs
15 ml (1 level tbsp) granulated
  sugar
few drops of vanilla flavouring

1 Pour the milk into a large measuring jug and microwave on HIGH for 2 minutes until hot.

2 Lightly whisk the eggs, sugar and vanilla flavouring together in a medium bowl. Add the heated milk, mix well and strain back into the jug.

3 Microwave on HIGH for 1 minute, then microwave on LOW for 4½ minutes or until the custard coats the back of a spoon thinly, whisking several times during cooking.
  N.B. the sauce thickens slightly on cooling.
  Serve hot or cold with sponge puddings or fruit.

JAM OR MARMALADE SAUCE

SERVES 4
100 g (4 oz) jam or marmalade,
  sieved if preferred
2.5 ml (½ level tsp) cornflour
few drops of lemon juice

1 Put the jam or marmalade and 150 ml (¼ pint) water in a medium bowl and microwave on HIGH for 2 minutes.

2 Blend the cornflour with 30 ml (2 tbsp) water then stir into the heated mixture.

3 Microwave on HIGH for 1–2 minutes until boiling, stirring after 1 minute.

4 Add lemon juice to taste, before serving.

APPLE SAUCE

MAKES ABOUT 300 ml (½ pint)
450 g (1 lb) cooking apples, peeled,
  cored and sliced
15 g (½ oz) butter
few drops of lemon juice
30 ml (2 tbsp) sugar

1 Put the apples in a medium bowl with the butter, lemon juice, sugar and 15 ml (1 tbsp) water. Cover with cling film, pulling back one corner to allow the steam to escape.

2 Microwave on HIGH for 6–8 minutes until the apples are soft.

3 Beat well until smooth, or sieve or liquidise in a blender or food processor.
Serve with pork or roast duck.

CHOCOLATE SAUCE

MAKES 300 ml (½ pint)
15 ml (1 level tbsp) cornflour
15 ml (1 level tbsp) cocoa powder
30 ml (2 level tbsp) sugar
300 ml (½ pint) milk
15 g (½ oz) butter

1 Put the cornflour, cocoa powder and sugar in a measuring jug or medium bowl and blend together with enough of the milk to give a smooth paste.

2 Stir in the remaining milk and the butter.

3 Microwave on HIGH for 3–4 minutes until the sauce has thickened, stirring every minute. Stir well and serve.

CUSTARD SAUCE

MAKES 568 ml (1 pint)
15–30 ml (1–2 level tbsp) sugar
30 ml (2 level tbsp) custard powder
  or 600 ml (1 pint) packet
568 ml (1 pint) milk

1 Blend the sugar and custard powder with a little of the milk in a measuring jug or medium bowl. Stir in the remaining milk.

2 Microwave the sauce on HIGH for 3–4 minutes or until thickened, stirring after every 2 minutes. Stir well and serve.

PRESERVES AND CONFECTIONERY

With a microwave cooker the lengthy, laborious boiling of dangerously hot saucepans normally required for making preserves and confectionery is a thing of the past. The cooking is quick, it is done in an enclosed space, ordinary heatproof bowls can be used instead of saucepans and they are very easy to clean afterwards. The bowls should, however, be handled with oven gloves as they become hot during the cooking due to the conduction of heat from the food.

Microwave cookers are particularly useful for preparing small quantities of preserves and confectionery that are so difficult to make by conventional methods because of the high risk of burning.

The jars that are to be used for preserves can be sterilised in the microwave oven. Quarter fill up to 4 jars with water arranged in a circle in the oven then bring to the boil on HIGH. Remove each jar as it is ready, wearing oven gloves, and pour out the water. Invert the jar on to a clean tea towel or absorbent kitchen paper and use when required.

Testing preserves for setting point

Place a small plate or saucer in the refrigerator before starting to make the preserve. When the preserve is ready to test for setting, drop a teaspoonful on to the saucer or plate, leave it to cool then gently push it with a finger. If the surface wrinkles the setting point has been reached. If it does not, return the preserve to the oven for one minute then re-test.

Covering preserves

After potting the preserve, cover the surface of the preserve with a disc of waxed paper then cover the jar with dampened jam pot covers and secure with tightly-tied string or elastic bands.

RASPBERRY JAM

MAKES 700 g (1½ lb)
450 g (1 lb) frozen raspberries
30 ml (2 tbsp) lemon juice
450 g (1 lb) granulated sugar
knob of butter

1 Put the frozen fruit in a large heatproof bowl and microwave on HIGH for 4 minutes to thaw. Stir several times with a wooden spoon to ensure even thawing.

2 Add the lemon juice and sugar. Mix well and microwave on HIGH for 5 minutes until the sugar has dissolved. Stir several times during cooking.

3 Add the butter and microwave on HIGH for 13 minutes, stirring occasionally, until setting point is reached. Remove any scum with a slotted spoon.

4 Leave to cool for 15 minutes to prevent the fruit rising in the jars. Pour into hot sterilised jars, cover and label.

STRAWBERRY JAM

MAKES 700 g (1½ lb)
450 g (1 lb) fresh strawberries,
  hulled
450 g (1 lb) granulated sugar
30 ml (2 tbsp) lemon juice
knob of butter

1 Gently mix the strawberries, sugar and lemon juice together in a large heatproof bowl. Cover tightly and leave to stand for 6–8 hours until the strawberries soften and a syrup is formed.

2 Microwave on LOW for 15 minutes until the sugar is completely dissolved. Stir very gently twice during cooking.

3 Add the knob of butter and microwave on HIGH for 25 minutes, stirring occasionally, until setting point is reached. Remove any scum with a slotted spoon.

4 Leave to cool for 15 minutes to prevent the fruit rising in the jars. Pour into hot sterilised jars, cover and label.

CHOCOLATE FUDGE

MAKES 36 SQUARES
100 g (4 oz) plain chocolate
100 g (4 oz) butter or margarine
450 g (1 lb) icing sugar
45 ml (3 tbsp) milk

1 Put the chocolate, butter, icing sugar and milk in a large heatproof bowl. Microwave on HIGH for 3 minutes until the chocolate has melted.

2 Beat vigorously with a wooden spoon until smooth.

3 Pour into a 20.5 × 15 cm (8 × 6 inch) rectangular container. Using a sharp knife mark lightly into squares. Leave in the refrigerator for 1–2 hours until set. Serve cut into squares.

LEMON CURD

MAKES 900 g (2 lb)
finely grated rind and juice of
  4 large lemons
4 eggs, beaten
225 g (8 oz) caster sugar
100 g (4 oz) butter, diced

1 Put the lemon rind in a large heatproof bowl. Mix the juice with the eggs and strain into the bowl. Stir in the sugar then add the butter.

2 Microwave on HIGH for 1 minute, stir, then microwave for 5 minutes until the lemon curd is thick. Whisk well every minute to prevent curdling.

3 Using oven gloves, remove the bowl from the oven and continue whisking until the mixture is cool. Lemon curd thickens on cooling.

4 Pour into hot sterilised jars. Cover, label and store in the refrigerator for up to 2–3 weeks.

ORANGE MARMALADE

MAKES 1.1 kg (2½ lb)
900 g (2 lb) Seville oranges
2 lemons
900 g (2 lb) granulated sugar
knob of butter

1 Pare the oranges, avoiding the white pith. Shred or chop the rind and set aside.

2 Put the fruit pith, flesh and pips in a food processor and chop until the pips are broken.

3 Put the chopped mixture into a large heatproof mixing bowl and add 900 ml (1½ pints) boiling water. Microwave on HIGH for 15 minutes.

4 Strain the mixture into another large heatproof bowl and press the cooked pulp until all the juice is squeezed out. Discard the pulp. Stir the shredded rind into the hot juice and microwave on HIGH for 15 minutes until the rind is tender, stirring occasionally. Stir in the sugar until dissolved. Cover the bowl with cling film, pulling back one corner to allow the steam to escape, and microwave on HIGH for 10 minutes.

5 Stir in the butter and microwave on HIGH for 5–6 minutes, stirring once during cooking, until setting point is reached. Remove any scum with a slotted spoon.

6 Leave to cool for 15 minutes to prevent the fruit rising in the jars. Pour into hot sterilised jars, cover and label.

TOMATO CHUTNEY

MAKES 900 g (2 lb)
700 g (1½ lb) firm tomatoes
225 g (8 oz) cooking apples, peeled and cored
1 medium onion, skinned
100 g (4 oz) soft dark brown sugar
100 g (4 oz) sultanas
5 ml (1 level tsp) salt
200 ml (7 fl oz) malt vinegar
15 g (½ oz) ground ginger
1.25 ml (¼ level tsp) cayenne pepper
2.5 ml (½ level tsp) mustard powder

1 Put the tomatoes in a large heatproof bowl and just cover with boiling water. Microwave on HIGH for 4 minutes, then lift the tomatoes out one by one using a slotted spoon and remove their skins.

2 Blend the apple and onion to a thick paste in a food processor. Roughly chop the tomatoes.

3 Mix all the ingredients together in a large heatproof bowl. Cover with cling film, pulling back one corner to allow the steam to escape, and microwave on HIGH for 45 minutes until the mixture is thick and has no excess liquid. Stir every 5 minutes during cooking and take particular care, stirring more frequently, during the last 5 minutes.

4 Leave to stand for 10 minutes, then stir. Pour into hot sterilised jars, cover and label.

GLOSSARY

THAWING MEAT

Frozen meat exudes a lot of liquid during defrosting and because microwaves are attracted to water, the liquid should be poured off or mopped up with absorbent kitchen paper when it collects, otherwise defrosting will take longer. Start defrosting a joint in its wrapper and remove it as soon as possible – usually after one-quarter of the defrosting time. Place the joint on a microwave roasting rack so that it does not stand in liquid during defrosting.

Remember to turn over a large piece of meat. If the joint shows signs of cooking give the meat a 'rest' period of 20 minutes. A joint is thawed when a skewer can easily pass through the thickest part of the meat. Chops and steaks should be re-positioned during defrosting; test them by pressing the surface with your fingers – the meat should feel cold to the touch and give in the thickest part.

Type	Approximate time on LOW	Special instructions
Beef		
Boned roasting joints (sirloin, topside)	8–10 minutes per 450 g (1 lb)	*Turn* over regularly during defrosting and rest if the meat shows signs of cooking. *Stand* for 1 hour.
Joints on bone (rib of beef)	10–12 minutes per 450 g (1 lb)	*Turn* over joint during defrosting. The meat will still be icy in the centre but will complete thawing if you leave it to stand for 1 hour.
Minced beef	8–10 minutes per 450 g (1 lb)	*Stand* for 10 minutes.
Cubed steak	6–8 minutes per 450 g (1 lb)	*Stand* for 10 minutes.
Steak (sirloin, rump)	8–10 minutes per 450 g (1 lb)	*Stand* for 10 minutes.
Beefburgers		
standard (50 g/2 oz)	2 burgers: 2 minutes 4 burgers: 2–3 minutes	Can be cooked from frozen, without defrosting, if preferred.
quarter-pounder	2 burgers: 2–3 minutes 4 burgers: 5 minutes	
burger buns	2 buns: 2 minutes	*Stand* burger buns for 2 minutes.
Lamb/Veal		
Boned rolled joint (loin, leg, shoulder)	5–6 minutes per 450 g (1 lb)	As for boned roasting joints of beef above. *Stand* for 30–45 minutes.
On the bone (leg and shoulder)	5–6 minutes per 450 g (1 lb)	As for beef joints on bone above. *Stand* for 30–45 minutes.
Minced lamb or veal	8–10 minutes per 450 g (1 lb)	*Stand* for 10 minutes.
Chops	8–10 minutes per 450 g (1 lb)	*Separate* during defrosting. *Stand* for 10 minutes.
Pork		
Boned rolled joint (loin, leg)	7–8 minutes per 450 g (1 lb)	As for boned roasting joints of beef above. *Stand* for 1 hour.
On the bone (leg, hand)	7–8 minutes per 450 g (1 lb)	As for beef joints on bone above. *Stand* for 1 hour.

Type	Approximate time on LOW	Special instructions
Tenderloin	8−10 minutes per 450 g (1 lb)	*Stand* for 10 minutes.
Chops	8−10 minutes per 450 g (1 lb)	*Separate* during defrosting and arrange 'spoke' fashion. *Stand* for 10 minutes.
Sausages	5−6 minutes per 450 g (1 lb)	*Separate* during defrosting. *Stand* for 5 minutes.
Offal		
Liver	8−10 minutes per 450 g (1 lb)	*Separate* during defrosting. *Stand* for 5 minutes.
Kidney	6−9 minutes per 450 g (1 lb)	*Separate* during defrosting. *Stand* for 5 minutes.

TIME AND SETTINGS FOR COOKING MEAT

Type	Time/Setting	Microwave Cooking Technique(s)
Beef		
Boned roasting joint (sirloin, topside)	per 450 g (1 lb) Rare: 5−6 minutes on HIGH Medium: 7−8 minutes on HIGH Well: 8−10 minutes on HIGH	*Turn* over joint halfway through cooking time. *Stand* for 15−20 minutes, tented in foil.
On the bone roasting joint (fore rib, back rib)	per 450 g (1 lb) Rare: 5 minutes on HIGH Medium: 6 minutes on HIGH Well: 8 minutes on HIGH	*Turn* over joint halfway through cooking time. *Stand* as for boned joint.
Lamb/Veal		
Boned rolled joint (loin, leg, shoulder)	per 450 g (1 lb) Medium: 7−8 minutes on HIGH Well: 8−10 minutes on HIGH	*Turn* over joint halfway through cooking time. *Stand* as for beef.
On the bone (leg and shoulder)	per 450 g (1 lb) Medium: 6−7 minutes on HIGH Well: 8−9 minutes on HIGH	*Position* fatty side down first and turn over halfway through cooking time. *Stands* as for beef.
Crown roast of lamb	9−10 minutes on MEDIUM per 450 g (1 lb) stuffed weight	*Re-position* partway through cooking time. *Stand* for 20 minutes with foil tenting.
Bacon		
Joints	12−14 minutes on HIGH per 450 g (1 lb)	*Cook* in a pierced roasting bag. *Turn* over joint partway through cooking time. *Stand* for 10 minutes, tented in foil.
Rashers	2 rashers: 2−2½ minutes on HIGH 4 rashers: 4−4½ minutes on HIGH 6 rashers: 5−6 minutes on HIGH	*Arrange* in a single layer. *Cover* with greaseproof paper to prevent spattering. *Cook* in preheated browning dish if liked. *Remove* paper immediately after cooking to prevent sticking. For large quantities:
	12 minutes on HIGH per 450 g (1 lb)	*Overlap* slices and place on microwave rack. *Re-position* three times during cooking.

Type	Time/Setting	Microwave Cooking Technique(s)
Offal		
Liver (lamb and calves)	6–8 minutes on HIGH per 450 g (1 lb)	*Cover* with greaseproof paper to prevent spattering.
Kidneys	8 minutes on HIGH per 450 g (1 lb)	*Arrange* in a circle *Cover* to prevent spattering. *Re-position* during cooking.
Chops	1½ minutes on HIGH, then 1½–2 minutes on MEDIUM	*Cook* in preheated browning dish. *Position* with bone ends towards centre.
Pork		
Boned rolled joint (loin, leg)	8–10 minutes on HIGH per 450 g (1 lb)	As for boned rolled lamb above.
On the bone (leg, hand)	8–9 minutes on HIGH per 450 g (1 lb)	As for lamb on the bone above.
Chops	1 chop: 4–4½ minutes on HIGH 2 chops: 5–5½ minutes on HIGH 3 chops: 6–7 minutes on HIGH 4 chops: 6½–8 minutes on HIGH	*Cook* in preheated browning dish. *Position* with bone ends towards centre. *Prick* kidney if attached. *Turn* over once during cooking.
Sausages	2 sausages: 2½ minutes on HIGH 4 sausages: 4 minutes on HIGH	*Pierce* skins. *Cook* in preheated browning dish. *Turn* occasionally during cooking.

THAWING POULTRY AND GAME

Poultry or game should be thawed in its freezer wrapping which should be pierced first and the metal tag removed. During defrosting, pour off liquid that collects in the bag. Finish defrosting in a bowl of cold water with the bird still in its bag. Cook all poultry immediately after thawing.

Type	Approximate time on LOW	Special instructions
Whole chicken or duckling	6–8 minutes per 450 g (1 lb)	Remove giblets. *Stand* in cold water for 30 minutes.
Whole turkey	10–12 minutes per 450 g (1 lb)	Remove giblets. *Stand* in cold water for 2–3 hours.
Chicken portions	5–7 minutes per 450 g (1 lb)	*Separate* during defrosting. *Stand* for 10 minutes.
Poussin, grouse, pheasant, pigeon, quail	5–7 minutes per 450 g (1 lb)	

TIME AND SETTINGS FOR COOKING POULTRY

Type	Time/Setting	Microwave Cooking Technique(s)
Chicken		
Whole chicken	8–10 minutes on HIGH per 450 g (1 lb)	*Cook* in a roasting bag, breast side down and turn halfway through cooking. *Brown* under conventional grill, if preferred. *Stand* for 10–15 minutes.
Portions	6–8 minutes on HIGH per 450 g (1 lb)	*Position* skin side up with thinner parts towards the centre. *Re-position* halfway through cooking time. *Stand* for 5–10 minutes.

Type	Time/Setting	Microwave Cooking Technique(s)
Chicken (cont.)		
Boneless breast	2–3 minutes on HIGH	Brown under grill, if preferred.
Duck		
Whole	7–10 minutes on HIGH per 450 g (1 lb)	Turn over as for whole chicken. Stand for 10–15 minutes.
Portions	4 × 300 g (11 oz) pieces: 10 minutes on HIGH, then 30–35 minutes on MEDIUM	Position and re-position as for chicken portions above.
Turkey		
Whole	9–11 minutes on HIGH per 450 g (1 lb)	Turn over 3–4 times, depending on size, during cooking; start cooking breast side down. Stand for 10–15 minutes.

THAWING FISH AND SHELLFISH

Separate fish cutlets, fillets or steaks as soon as possible during defrosting. Like poultry, it is best to finish defrosting whole fish in cold water to prevent drying out of the surface. Arrange scallops and prawns in a circle and cover with absorbent kitchen paper to help absorb liquid; remove pieces from the cooker as soon as defrosted.

Type	Approximate time on LOW	Special instructions
White fish fillets or cutlets, e.g. cod, coley, haddock, halibut, or whole plaice or sole	3–4 minutes per 450 g (1 lb) plus 2–3 minutes.	Stand for 5 minutes after each 2–3 minutes.
Oily fish, e.g. whole and gutted mackerel,	2–3 minutes per 225 g (8 oz) plus 3–4 minutes	Stand for 5 minutes between defrosts and for 5 minutes afterwards.
Kipper fillets	2–3 minutes per 225 g (8 oz)	As for oily fish above.
Lobster tails, crab claws, etc.	3–4 minutes per 225 g (8 oz) plus 2–3 minutes	As for oily fish above.
Prawns, shrimps, scampi	2½ minutes per 100 g (4 oz) 3–4 minutes per 225 g (8 oz)	Pierce plastic bag if necessary. Stand for 2 minutes. Separate with a fork after 2 minutes. Stand for 2 minutes, then plunge into cold water and drain.

TIME AND SETTINGS FOR COOKING FISH IN THE MICROWAVE

Type	Time/Setting	Microwave Cooking Technique(s)
Whole round fish (whiting, mullet, trout. carp, bream, small haddock)	3 minutes on HIGH per 450 g (1 lb)	Slash skin to prevent bursting Turn over fish partway through cooking time. Re-position fish if cooking more than 2.
Whole flat fish (plaice, sole)	3 minutes on HIGH	Slash skin. Turn dish partway through cooking time.
Cutlets, steaks, fillets	4 minutes on HIGH per 450 g (1 lb)	Position thicker parts towards the outside, overlapping thin ends and separating with cling film or foil. Turn over fillets and quarter-turn dish 3 times during cooking.

THAWING BAKED GOODS AND PASTRY DOUGH

To absorb the moisture of thawing cakes, breads and pastry, place them on absorbent kitchen paper (remove as soon as defrosted to prevent sticking). For greater crispness, place baked goods and the paper on a microwave rack or elevate food on an upturned bowl to allow the air to circulate underneath.

Type	Quantity	Approximate time on LOW setting	Special instructions
Bread			
Loaf, whole	1 large	6–8 minutes	Uncover and place on absorbent
Loaf, whole	1 small	4–6 minutes	kitchen paper.
			Turn over during defrosting.
			Stand for 5–15 minutes.
Loaf, sliced	1 large	6–8 minutes	*Defrost* in original wrapper but
Loaf, sliced	1 small	4–6 minutes	remove any metal tags.
			Stand for 10–15 minutes.
Slice of bread	25 g (1 oz)	10–15 seconds	*Place* on absorbent kitchen paper.
			Time carefully.
			Stand for 1–2 minutes.
Bread rolls, tea-cakes,	2	15–20 seconds	*Place* on absorbent kitchen paper.
scones, etc.	4	25–35 seconds	*Time* carefully.
			Stand for 2–3 minutes.
Crumpets	2	15–20 seconds	As for bread rolls above.
Cakes and Pastries			
Cakes	2 small	30–60 seconds	*Place* on absorbent kitchen paper.
	4 small	1–1½ minutes	*Stand* for 5 minutes.
Sponge cake	450 g (1 lb)	1–1½ minutes	*Place* on absorbent kitchen paper.
			Test and turn after 1 minute.
			Stand for 5 minutes.
Jam doughnuts	2	45–60 seconds	*Place* on absorbent kitchen paper.
	4	45–90 seconds	*Stand* for 5 minutes.
Cream doughnuts	2	45–60 seconds	*Place* on absorbent kitchen paper.
	4	1¼–1¾ minutes	*Check* after half the defrosting time.
			Stand for 10 minutes.
Cream éclairs	2	45 seconds	*Stand* for 5–10 minutes.
	4	1–1½ minutes	*Stand* for 15–20 minutes.
Choux buns	4 small	1–1½ minutes	*Stand* for 20–30 minutes.
Pastry			
Shortcrust and puff	227 g (8 oz) packet	1 minute	*Stand* for 20 minutes.
	397 g (14 oz) packet	2 minutes	*Stand* for 20–30 minutes.

THAWING DESSERTS

Type	Approximate time on LOW	Special instructions
Cheesecake with fruit topping	about 3–4 minutes for 23 cm (9 inch) diameter cheesecake	*Place* on serving dish. *Stand* for 20 minutes.
Fruit pie	4–5 minutes for 650 g (26 oz) pie	*Stand* for 5–10 minutes. *Do not* make on a metal tin.
Mousse	30 seconds per individual mousse	*Remove* lid before defrosting. *Stand* for 15–20 minutes.
Trifle	45–60 seconds per individual trifle	*Remove* lid before defrosting. *Stand* for 15–20 minutes.

TIME AND SETTINGS FOR RICE AND PASTA

Although there are no real time savings in cooking rice and pasta in the microwave, it may be a more foolproof way of cooking. Add boiling water to come at least 2.5 cm (1 inch) above the rice. Drain after the standing time.

Dried peas and beans are not recommended for microwaving. The skins remain tough and will burst during cooking. Split lentils, however, can be successfully microwaved because they are not completely encased in a skin.

Type and quantity	Time on HIGH setting	Microwave cooking technique(s)
White long grain rice 225 g (8 oz)	10–12 minutes	*Stir* once during cooking. *Stand* for 10 minutes.
350 g (12 oz)	12–14 minutes	
Brown rice, 100 g (4 oz)	30 minutes	As for white long grain rice.
Pasta shapes, 225 g (8 oz) dried	7 minutes	*Stir* once during cooking. *Stand* for 5 minutes.
Spaghetti, tagliatelli, 225 g (8 oz) dried	7–8 minutes	*Stand* for 10 minutes.
350 g (12 oz) dried	8–10 minutes	

FROZEN VEGETABLES COOKING CHART

Frozen vegetables may be cooked straight from the freezer. Many may be cooked in their original plastic packaging or pouch, as long as it is first slit and then placed on a plate. Alternatively transfer to a bowl.

Vegetable	Quantity	Approximate time on HIGH	Microwave Cooking Technique(s)
Asparagus	275 g (10 oz)	7–9 minutes	*Separate* and re-arrange after 3 minutes.
Beans, Broad	225 g (8 oz)	7–8 minutes	*Stir* or *shake* during cooking period.
Beans, Green cut	225 g (8 oz)	6–8 minutes	*Stir* or *shake* during cooking period.
Broccoli	275 g (10 oz)	7–9 minutes	*Re-arrange* spears after 3 minutes.
Brussels sprouts	225 g (8 oz)	6–8 minutes	*Stir* or *shake* during cooking period.
Cauliflower florets	275 g (10 oz)	7–9 minutes	*Stir* or *shake* during cooking period.
Carrots	225 g (8 oz)	6–7 minutes	*Stir* or *shake* during cooking period.
Corn-on-the-cob	1	3–4 minutes	*Do not* add water. Dot with butter, wrap in greaseproof paper.
	2	6–7 minutes	
Mixed vegetables	225 g (8 oz)	5–6 minutes	*Stir* or *shake* during cooking period.
Peas	225 g (8 oz)	5–6 minutes	*Stir* or *shake* during cooking period.
Peas and Carrots	225 g (8 oz)	7–8 minutes	*Stir* or *shake* during cooking period.
Spinach, Leaf or Chopped	275 g (10 oz)	7–9 minutes	*Do not* add water. *Stir* or *shake* during cooking period.
Swede/Turnip, diced	225 g (8 oz)	6–7 minutes	*Stir* or *shake* during cooking period. *Mash* with butter after standing time.
Sweetcorn	225 g (8 oz)	4–6 minutes	*Stir* or *shake* during cooking period.

TIME AND SETTINGS FOR FRESH VEGETABLES

Vegetables need very little water added when microwaved. When using these charts add 30 ml (2 tbsp) water unless otherwise stated. In this way they retain their colour, flavour and nutrients more than they would if cooked conventionally. They can be cooked in boiling bags, plastic containers and polythene bags — pierce the bag before cooking to make sure there is a space for steam to escape.

Prepare vegetables in the normal way. It is most important that food is cut to an even size and stems are of the same length. Vegetables with skins, such as aubergines, need to be pierced before microwaving to prevent bursting. Season vegetables with salt after cooking. Salt distorts the microwave patterns and dries the vegetables.

Vegetable	Quantity	Approximate time on HIGH	Microwave Cooking Technique(s)
Artichoke, Globe	1	5–6 minutes	*Place* upright in covered dish.
	2	7–8 minutes	
	3	11–12 minutes	
	4	12–13 minutes	
Asparagus	450 g (1 lb)	7–8 minutes	*Place* stalks towards the outside of the dish. *Re-position* during cooking.
Aubergine	450 g (1 lb) 0.5 cm (¼'') slices	5–6 minutes	*Stir* or *shake* after 4 minutes.
Beans, Broad	450 g (1 lb)	6–8 minutes	*Stir* or *shake* after 3 minutes and test after 5 minutes.
Beans, Green	450 g (1 lb) sliced into 2.5 cm (1'') lengths	10–13 minutes	*Stir* or *shake* during the cooking period. Time will vary with age.
Beetroot, whole	4 medium	14–16 minutes	*Pierce* skin with a fork. *Re-position* during cooking.
Broccoli	450 g (1 lb) small florets	7–8 minutes	*Re-position* during cooking. *Place* stalks towards the outside of the dish.
Brussels sprouts	225 g (8 oz) 450 g (1 lb)	4–6 minutes 7–10 minutes	*Stir* or *shake* during cooking.
Cabbage	450 g (1 lb) quartered 450 g (1 lb) shredded	8 minutes 8–10 minutes	*Stir* or *shake* during cooking.
Carrots	450 g (1 lb) small whole 450 g (1 lb) 0.5 cm (¼'') slices	8–10 minutes 9–12 minutes	*Stir* or *shake* during cooking.
Cauliflower	whole 450 g (1 lb) 225 g (8 oz) florets 450 g (1 lb) florets	9–12 minutes 5–6 minutes 7–8 minutes	*Stir* or *shake* during cooking.
Celery	450 g (1 lb) sliced into 2.5 cm (1'') lengths	8–10 minutes	*Stir* or *shake* during cooking.
Corn-on-the-cob	2 (450 g (1 lb))	6–7 minutes	*Wrap* individually in buttered greaseproof paper. *Do not* add water. *Turn* over after 3 minutes.
Courgettes	450 g (1 lb) 2.5 cm (1'') slices	5–7 minutes	*Do not* add more than 30 ml (2 tbsp) water. *Stir* or *shake* gently twice during cooking. *Stand* for 2 minutes before draining.

Vegetable	Quantity	Approximate time on HIGH	Microwave Cooking Technique(s)
Fennel	450 g (1 lb) 0.5 cm (¼″) slices	7–9 minutes	*Stir* and *shake* during cooking.
Leeks	450 g (1 lb) 2.5 cm (1″) slices	6–8 minutes	*Stir* or *shake* during cooking.
Mange Tout	450 g (1 lb)	7–9 minutes	
Mushrooms	225 g (8 oz) whole 450 g (1 lb) whole	2–3 minutes 5 minutes	*Do not* add water. Add 25 g (1 oz) butter and a squeeze of lemon juice. *Stir* or *shake* gently during cooking.
Onions	225 g (8 oz) thinly sliced 450 g (1 lb) small whole	7–8 minutes 9–11 minutes	*Stir* or *shake* sliced onions. *Add* only 60 ml (4 tbsp) water to whole onions. *Re-position* whole onions during cooking.
Okra	450 g (1 lb) whole	6–8 minutes	
Parsnips	450 g (1 lb) (halved)	10–16 minutes	*Place* thinner parts towards the centre. *Add* a knob of butter and 15 ml (1 tbsp) lemon juice with 150 ml (¼ pint) water. *Turn* dish during cooking and *re-position*.
Peas	450 g (1 lb)	9–11 minutes	*Stir* or *shake* during cooking.
Potatoes			*Wash* and prick the skin with a fork.
Baked jacket	1 × 175 g (6 oz) potato 2 × 175 g (6 oz) potatoes 4 × 175 g (6 oz) potatoes	4–6 minutes 6–8 minutes 12–14 minutes	*Place* on absorbent kitchen paper or napkin. When cooking more than 2 at a time, arrange in a circle. *Turn* over halfway through cooking.
Boiled (old) halved	450 g (1 lb)	7–10 minutes	*Add* 60 ml (4 tbsp) water. *Stir* or *shake* during cooking.
Boiled (new) whole	450 g (1 lb)	6–9 minutes	*Add* 60 ml (4 tbsp) water. *Do not* overcook or new potatoes become spongy.
Sweet	450 g (1 lb)	5 minutes	*Wash* and prick the skin with a fork. *Place* on absorbent kitchen paper. *Turn* over halfway through cooking time.
Spinach	450 g (1 lb) chopped	5–6 minutes	*Do not* add water. Best cooked in roasting bag, sealed with non-metal fastening. *Stir* or *Shake* during cooking.
Swede	450 g (1 lb) 1.5 cm (¾″) dice	11–13 minutes	*Stir* or *shake* during cooking.
Turnip	450 g (1 lb) 1.5 cm (¾″) dice	9–11 minutes	*Add* 60 ml (4 tbsp) water and *stir* or *shake* during cooking.

INDEX